The Ultima
Counterterrorist
Home Companion

Six Incapacitating Holds
Involving a Spatula and Other
Ways to Protect Your Family

Zack Arnstein and Larry Arnstein

Illustrations by Bryan Duddles

SANTA
MONICA
PRESS

S A N T A
M O N I C A
P R E S S

Published by: Santa Monica Press LLC
P.O. Box 1076
Santa Monica, CA 90406-1076
1-800-784-9553
www.santamonicapress.com
books@santamonicapress.com

Printed in the United States

Santa Monica Press books are available at special quantity discounts when purchased in bulk by corporations, organizations, or groups. Please call our Special
Sales department at 1-800-784-9553.

ISBN-13 978-1-59580-025-1
ISBN-10 1-59580-025-5

Library of Congress Cataloging-in-Publication Data

Arnstein, Zack, 1980–
The ultimate counterterrorist home companion : six incapacitating holds involv-
ing a spatula and other ways to protect your family / by Zack Arnstein and Larry
Arnstein.
      p. cm.
   Includes bibliographical references.
   ISBN-13: 978-1-59580-025-1
   ISBN-10: 1-59580-025-5
   1. Terrorism—Humor. 2. Terrorism—Prevention—Humor. I. Arnstein, Larry,
1945- II. Title.

PN6231.T555A76 2007
818'.607—dc22
2007025918

Cover and interior design and production by cooldogdesign
Illustrations by Bryan Duddles

Contents

The Building Blocks of the Core Principles

Chapter 1

Why Terrorism Is a Bigger Threat Than Any Threat Any Nation Has Ever Faced in the History of the World, Ever

9/11 has changed everything. No longer can America live in the peaceful culture of mutual respect that we have been blessed with since the beginning of our nation.

There is pre-9/11 thinking, and there is post-9/11 thinking. They are as different as It's a Small World at Disneyland, and Pirates of the Caribbean at Disneyland. Before 9/11 we used to be concerned about simple things like which weed killer to use on our lawns, underarm odor, and nuclear war with Russia. Now, we have a real enemy, intent on killing innocent Americans. All that whimsical pillow talk about barbecues on the front lawn, leaving the door unlocked all day, civil liberties, checks and balances, and universal suffrage that we were once so fond of must now be reconsidered.

We are more afraid than ever about terrorism, and rightfully so. As you can see in the following chart, terrorism has risen to become one of the Most Leading Causes of Death in

Most Leading Causes of Death in America

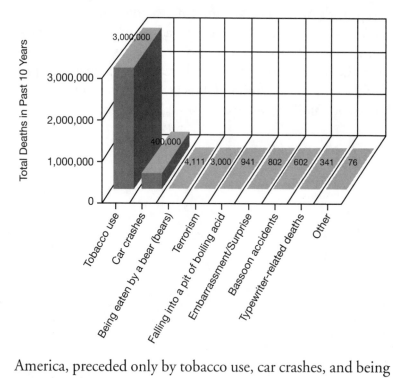

America, preceded only by tobacco use, car crashes, and being eaten by a bear.

Note that in order to make a nice-looking chart, we have understated the number of deaths caused by tobacco use by a factor of 10. Also, some of the other statistics on bears, boiling acid pits, and typewriter-related deaths are approximate, based on anecdotal evidence, hearsay, common sense, and rumor.

So clearly Americans have good reason to be fearful. Fear is a natural reaction to the anticipation or presence of danger. When we hear the talk about WMD, when we see our terror alert levels raised, when we hear that guy from *Friends* who plays Joey is going to be in a new movie, it's only natural to get scared. But we don't have to live in fear anymore. It's time to fight back. It's time to prepare. It's time we tell that guy from *Friends* that we won't see any more of his movies, although we did enjoy the time we spent watching *Friends*.

In this book we'll talk about the role of our government, and provide other generally informative information. But you don't want to spend a lot of time reading while your home is vulnerable to terrorists. Let's not lose focus before we gain focus. Let's get you and your family ready and prepared by presenting some of the building blocks of the core principles of home and family counterterrorism. Here we go, and we're off!

Chapter 2

Planning Your Family Antiterrorism Drill: What to Do When Little Lucy Can't Assemble Her Matador 25B Anti-tank Rocket Launcher in under 37 Seconds

Dad comes home from work, opens the door, steps on a toy truck your youngest son left in the living room, and goes flying into the wall, where he cuts his arm. You hear a voice from upstairs of a child saying the toilet is overflowing and water is pouring all over the bathroom and getting into the hallway. Your daughter screams from her room that she has a date in 25 minutes and she just broke a nail—that's when you decide to call an immediate antiterrorism drill. Why? Because you're a good captain of the house, and you know that terrorists don't strike only when it's convenient for you and your family. They don't strike when all appliances are functioning normally, when people are standing upright and ready, when nails are healthy and well groomed. They strike when you least expect it, and you have to be ready no matter what. Everyone to your posts!!

Running an antiterrorism drill can be confusing, and most people have a lot of questions. In this chapter we'll answer the most common of your questions: Is it under the desk or stop, drop, and roll? Into the basement or up to the roof? Over the rainbow or *Inside Sports*? Boxers or briefs? For here or to go? And any other questions you might be asking as long as they come in an either/or format.

Q: *When?*

A: Soon.

But first let's get back to those emergency posts. When we last discussed this topic 11 lines ago, you were on your way to your posts. But you don't know where you're going, do you? You got too excited, and ran your Antiterrorism Drill before finishing this chapter. That's OK, it's better to be too eager than not eager enough. Make sure someone in your family is assigned to each of the following posts (fig. 1).

Fig. 1. Emergency Posts

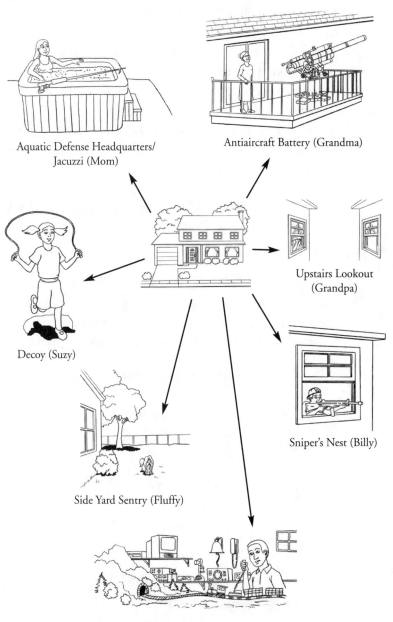

Aquatic Defense Headquarters/
Jacuzzi (Mom)

Antiaircraft Battery (Grandma)

Decoy (Suzy)

Upstairs Lookout
(Grandpa)

Sniper's Nest (Billy)

Side Yard Sentry (Fluffy)

Underground Command Central/Model
Train Area (Dad)

Making Your Terror Drill Kid Friendly

In the event of a chemical weapons release, you'll want to make sure your children are not afraid to put on their gas masks, or afraid to talk to you while you are wearing yours. For this reason, we suggest playing the "Snorgels" game. In the Snorgels game the whole family puts on their masks, talks in silly Snorgel voices, and jumps up and down (fig. 2).

This way, when the terrorists strike, instead of saying, "Everyone quick: put on your gas masks," you can say, "Everyone quick: let's play Snorgels!"

Q: You still haven't answered the questions you promised you would answer earlier in this chapter.

A: That's not a question.

Q: When are you going to answer those questions?

A: You're still thinking inside the box. The answers will come when you don't expect them, they could come from above, from below, or in your mailbox. You *must* be prepared.

Fig. 2. The Snorgels Game

Chapter 3

Hand-to-Hand Combat: Actually Fighting Terrorists in Your Living Room—Six Incapacitating Holds Involving a Spatula

A likely scenario: you just couldn't face the dinner dishes last night, and now, after breakfast, you've finally got everything into the dishwasher and turned it on, only to have a flood of filthy water pouring onto the kitchen floor. So you had to call the appliance repair shop, and sure enough, you find out your warranty just expired the day before yesterday, the repair involves an expensive replacement part, plus labor (coming to an estimated $892.27), and the repair guy they sent turns out to be a terrorist, and you just let him into your kitchen.

Luckily you have this chapter to study, so you're well-equipped to handle the threat posed by the "repair man," Mr. Mohammed.

At least you thought he said "Mohammed." He might have been saying, "More ham." But it doesn't matter now, it's all over for him, Mohammed, Mahoney, or Morgenstern. What matters is the 15 Most Sanitary Methods to Dispose of a Body, Leaving Your Kitchen Floor Blood-Free and Sparklingly Clean!

Message of Religious Tolerance: Not all Muslims want to sneak into your house at night, slit your throat, bathe their hands in your blood, and murder your family!

Message of Ethnic Tolerance: Not all Arabs are Muslim! There are Christian Arabs also. And lots of African-American Muslims with impressively good posture and very little neck movement. Also, not all Arab Muslims are terrorists! But enough heavy thinking. Let's get back to hand-to-hand combat!

The 13 Points of Death

These are definitionally quite deadly and should only be used in self-defense, preemptive self-defense, preventive attack, temporary insanity, and any time it seems apropos. These points of death may also be used for stress relief, relaxation, and therapeutic massage, but be careful!

13 Points of Death

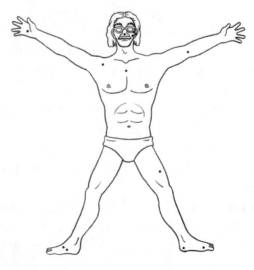

The Basic Restraining Holds

It is a truism that the efficacy of most, if not all, of the standard incapacitating holds that you will be using is substantially increased employing the use of an enabling object. But you cannot always expect to have access to your weapon of choice. In that crucial moment of a surprise attack, you must be able to perform these basic holds using whatever you can get your hands on.

The most commonly available enabling object used in terrorist home attack situations is the spatula. The spatula is a must-have for all kitchens, equally effective for basting, flipping, turning, straining, and defending your home against Global Islamic Jihadism. But there are all sorts of different spatulas designed specifically to cope with the requirements of the varied kinds of food preparation and physical assaults you will be facing.

We know you already know the standard holds, because if you didn't you'd probably already be dead. But how do you make the standard holds you already know more effective with the use of a spatula, and which spatula to choose?

Good question.

Effective Incapacitating Holds and Their Corresponding Spatula Complements

Incapacitating Hold Involving a Spatula	Recommended Spatula
Spatula Chin Lock 	*The Curved Silicon Spatula*—Pull up on the chin more effectively using this industry standard, also known as the "spoonula." The spoonula is great for scooping, scraping, stirring, as well as pummeling, pounding, pelting, and,

Incapacitating Hold Involving a Spatula	**Recommended Spatula**

Spatula Chin Lock (cont'd.)

of course, walloping and bludgeoning. A silicone spatula also has a very high melting point and will not be nicked or warped due to hot pans or friction from squirming.

Spatula Arm Bar

The Fish Turner—Upgrade your tired old arm bar with this handy tool normally used solely for cooking seafood but which can also help in cutting off blood circulation and airflow to the brain. A hole in the handle facilitates hanging on a peg, hook, or gun rack.

Spatula Front Sleeper

The Viper Straight Shaft—Get that crucial extra squeeze out of your Front Sleeper hold with this reinforced nylon beauty. If your kitchen has a particular color scheme, you can choose the right Viper to complement as it comes in green, blue, frosted yellow, frosted pink, and brown. Nylon is also soft and pliable, which means it will maintain its original shape in even some of the most intense combat/cooking situations.

Incapacitating Hold Involving a Spatula

Recommended Spatula

Spatula Claw Hold

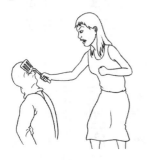

The Slotted Spatula—This bad boy has a plurality of drainage slots extended through the spatula head member, which are provided substantially transversely between the spatula head lateral sides. And that is obviously a good thing when performing a claw hold, and/or serving a mango chicken sauté.

Spatula Side Headlock

The Tiger 5000—The difference between a standard side headlock and one employing the power of a Tiger 5000 is unquestionable. This is a remarkably versatile unit for the fulfillment of countless objectives, both culinary and self-defense in nature. It's also a generous size for your big pots, pans, and terrorist adversaries.

Spatula Full Nelson

The Icing Knife—To improve a standard full nelson you're really looking for a no-nonsense, no-frills kind of spatula/antiterrorist enabler. Aside from the intimidating name, the Icing Knife spreads frosting like no other, and generally produces a more professional and smoothly finished cake. And because it's made of steel you can stab people in the heart with it.

Thinking Like a Warrior

Whenever you enter a room, consider possible escape routes, greatest potential threats, and whom you will kill first should you be attacked. Say you enter a potentially dangerous situation like this. What are your options, what are your kill priorities?

Potential Threats

! = High Threat (kill first)

? = Medium Threat (kill if necessary)

☺ = Low Threat (kill last)

→ = Escape Route

The second and final step in your warriorification process is to hone all your terror-fighting senses to the point where you can honestly refer to yourself in social situations as:

A One-Man/Woman Terror-Fighting Machine

Q: Is that like some kind of transgender thing?

A: Maybe we should have said "man or woman." Or "person" would have been more clear.

Q: Person would be awkward.

A: The fact that you have to use gender-specific nouns is a problem with English that you don't have in other languages, and now that you've wasted all our time on this, we're only going to have time for honing one sense: your sense of taste.

A sophisticated palate should be able to gauge the threat level of any room simply by tasting it. Instead of the junk you usually eat, exercise your palate by sampling the various exotic cuisines of other nations, like France, Thailand, and the Scandinavian countries (Denmark, Sweden, and Brazil.) Anyway, the point is: don't be too reliant on just your eyes. You need to have all your other faculties on alert. (Jesus gave you a nose: use it!)

Strategic Weapons Placement

You're about to be held hostage by a terrorist, but you're going to be just fine because you thought ahead. You've placed weapons strategically throughout your home that are easily accessible in the event of a hostile takeover. Of course, most terrorists are not likely to respond positively to: "OK, I'll be right there, just let me get my shotgun from the garage." But due to your strategic weapons placement, you can be more subtle.

You: OK, I'll be right there, let me just get a cookie.

That sounds reasonable enough. Plus, terrorists like cookies, so he'll be hoping you'll bring him one too. What a surprise when you return with a lethal weapon instead!

You: While we're sitting here waiting for you to get the ransom money, and for our government to agree to your demands, would you mind if I read aloud from the *Oxford English Dictionary?*
You: Do you mind if I change the kitty litter?

Speaking of kitty litter, let's take a little bathroom break. We'll reconvene in 10 minutes at Chapter 4.

Chapter 4

Places You Can No Longer Go: Airports, Stadiums, Outside

Outside is just not a safe place anymore like it used to be when the mafia ran things, and all you had to do to protect your family was keep quiet and give a healthy portion of your barber shop's profit to the big Italian guy with all the acne scars whose name invariably ended in a vowel. Now, going outside requires a lot more thought and forehead wrinkling. There are terrorists to think about, people who look like terrorists, people who you went to high school with who want to sell you anti-aging face wash, terrorists who want to sell you anti-aging face wash, and people who look like terrorists who want to be judged by the content of their character.

In this chapter we will make a persuasive argument for why it's really not a good idea to go outside anymore (and that includes rooms with windows). And that also includes rooms that share a wall with the outside. And by wall we also mean roof, so upstairs is out too.

But that doesn't necessarily mean you have to feel "trapped" inside your house or apartment. There are many satisfying alternatives to outside which we'll explore. For example: travel magazines. Another, quite different alternative is travel TV shows. And here's an idea for the particularly adventurous:

travel posters. In fact, not going outside anymore might be the most broadening experience of your life!

On the other hand, there are safer and less safe travel shows to watch.

Safe Travel Shows	Less Safe Travel Shows
The Cheeses of Northern Italy Adventure Tour	Searching For the Spot-Bellied Toad in the Warlord-Controlled Areas of Afghanistan
Spa/Wellness Swedish Excursion	Unarmed Camping in Southern Sudan
Great Lodges of the Canadian Rockies	Kurdistan: Twilight of a Civilization

Q: What could be unsafe about watching a travel show?

A: In a travel show you are metaphorically whisked away to a foreign land. What is safe about being metaphorically whisked to a place where the national sport is "Throw the Tourist From the Bridge"?

Q: How do I know if I'm outside or inside?

A: Outside tends to be breezy relative to inside. There are walls outside, but they are outside walls, whereas the walls on the inside are inside walls. Outside tends to have things like cars, clouds, and trees.

Q: I think I'm inside, but there seems to be a tree.

A: Then you're probably outside. You should get inside as quickly as possible.

Q: What if I have to go to the bathroom?

A: Remember, dogs are the ones that "go to the bathroom" outside. You should use the bathroom in your home, hence the phrase "go to the bathroom."

Moving along: in the title of this chapter we promised to talk about stadiums, and we will. Which brings us to the larger question of sports, specifically: cricket.

Cricket is the Number One favorite terrorist sport, causing several wars between Pakistan and India, so you should avoid attending cricket matches.

Q: Can you really classify any event during which you take an extended tea break a sport?

A: They throw a ball back and forth, somebody tries to hit the ball with some kind of bat, and some of them wear knee pads.

Q: But they break for tea.

A: Point taken. But cricket is an athletic-type event, and it's favored by terrorists, so don't go.

Q: I would never go to a cricket match under any circumstances.

A: Also, it's played outside (for more information on outside, see above).

Q: On the other hand, never going to stadiums? That could be tough. My children and I love to watch sports live. There's just nothing like it. What am I to do?

A: The point of saying stadiums are places you can no longer go is not to scare you out of ever attending a live sporting event again—that would just be unreasonable. However, terrorists are interested in targets that attract large masses of people. How about checking out a local Clippers game instead of the Lakers? Or the Kings instead of the Ducks? The Clippers and the Kings are both terrible teams who should probably be playing in the minor leagues instead of the NBA and NHL, respectively, and more important, the crowds are much smaller. Trade in the Kobe jersey for a Cuttino Mobely, buy the kids a hot dog, make sure they are playing a real team, and have a blast.

Q: But I hate the Clippers.

A: Well if you like not being dead more than you hate the Clippers, you'll find a way to get used to it.

Chapter 5

If Your Child Brings Home a Suspicious Playmate

Let's be absolutely clear on one thing: we do not in any way condone "racial profiling," or any kind of discrimination based on race, religion, or ethnicity, or any other kind of filing for that matter, be it taxes, for bankruptcy, or into line. So when we use the word "suspicious," we refer only to actions and attitudes in your child's playmate which trigger a "yellow flag," causing you to say, "Rebwar, come here. We need to talk."

Once Rebwar has been isolated, you must ask him politely to remove his shoes and hand over his backpack for a thorough inspection. If you find no explosive devices, you may proceed to the interrogation phase of your screening process. If Rebwar is a very young child, you should be careful not to frighten him, otherwise he's likely to "clam up," and you'll get nowhere. Start with a few friendly inquiries about how he likes school or summer camp or whatever, before venturing, "I see you have a copy of the Koran in your backpack. How nice! We all respect other religions in our family. How do you feel about *jihad?*"

Of course, there are other, gently probing questions to ask little Rebwar.

"Do you have any older brothers, Rebwar?"

"What have you heard about *jihad* from them?"

Most five- and six-year-olds are fidgety, and can't focus for very long on one thing, so it's best to break up the interrogation into several sessions, interspersed with playtime activities and milk and cookies. And it's not a bad idea to reward the child with extra cookies for any valuable tidbits he provides about his family. Using these techniques, you'll be surprised how easy it is to build up an impressive dossier on Rebwar and his entire network!

When your child is playing with a suspicious playmate, observe their play for clues. Do they play Cowboys and Indians, Cops and Robbers, or Crusaders and Warriors of the Holy Martyrs Brigade? Who has to be the Crusader?

When the rules suddenly get changed, as they often do in the silly games children play, what are the changes?

Good Change	Bad Change
No do-overs.	Losers must have their hands and feet cut off on opposite sides.
My shield now blocks lasers.	Winner gets all the virgins.
The Princess gets to ride both ponies.	Nonbelievers will be stoned to death.

Your child and his friend have been spending all day locked up in their clubhouse in the oak tree throwing things at passersby, healthy enough. But what are they calling their club? And what are their club activities?

Good Name for Club	Bad Name for Club
The Chaos Commandos (No Girls Allowed)	World Islamic Front for *Jihad* Against Jews and Crusaders (No Girls Allowed)
The Water Balloon Warriors	The Army for the Liberation of Holy Places and the Restoration of the Caliphate

Good Club Activities

Taking "top secret" pictures of neighbor Suzy for Uncle Charles.

Putting dirt and mud in people's food when they're not looking.

Bad Club Activities

Taking "top secret" pictures of bridges for Uncle Hashmat.

Overthrowing the diabolical Jewish usurious monetary system when they're not looking.

Jibby   Koko

Kidz Korner

Speaking of children, one of our primary goals in writing this book is to make counterterrorism appealing, accessible (and fun!) for children. On the lecture circuit we've been accused of being very serious and boring. Not so! Throughout this book we'll present games, puzzles, and other kid-friendly counterterrorist learning opportunities, while certainly not forgetting the fatal, grave nature of the threat to you and your children.

First off, we'd like you to meet a couple of our friends: this is Jibby, the Antiterrorist Bunny and his best friend Koko, the Surveillance and Reconnaissance Kangaroo.

They can be your friends too, if you like. So keep an eye out for them, they'll be hopping in and out of this book!

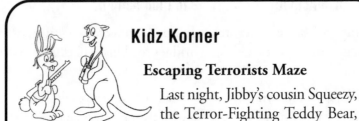

Kidz Korner

Escaping Terrorists Maze

Last night, Jibby's cousin Squeezy, the Terror-Fighting Teddy Bear, called Jibby for help. You see, Squeezy runs a terrorist detention center in the north end of the woods, and the terrorists are escaping! Jibby and Koko need to get quickly through the terrorist-infested woods to help Squeezy! Can you help them find the way?

Chapter 6

Hostage Negotiation: What to Get for the Terrorist Who Has Everything

Hostage negotiation (in the case of Islamic terrorism) is a much different process than Americans are accustomed to dealing with in their everyday lives. Unless you happen to have on hand more than 72 virgins, there's really very little you can offer someone who genuinely believes they are off to paradise as soon as the dynamite they strapped to their chest goes off.

So a better question really is, how does one not negotiate with terrorists? Try this technique:

You: Sorry, you must be going through a tunnel! (Make fake static sound.) You keep cutting in and out! Damn cell phones. You'll have to call back some other time.

Or this:

You: Thank you for calling our Hostage Negotiation Crisis Line. Your call is important to us. All of our operators are currently assisting other terrorists. Remember, you can get most of your demands met at no charge at www.hostagenegotiationcrisisline.com. If you would like to speak with one of our hostage negotiators, please stay on the line, and your call will be answered in the order in which it was received. Thank you for calling!

Getting Your Kids Back at Any Cost: Is It Worth It?

If you actually decide that you are willing to negotiate—because the terrorist has a hostage of sufficient value, like one of your children—here are some tips that will be helpful.

Do: Know what you're willing to pay before you open the negotiation. Estimate the monetary value of the child in question. What is your walk-away number? Is it the son who is good at baseball or the one that tends to fall a lot when playing baseball? This could sway your bottom line $100,000 one way or the other. If it's a girl, knock off $200,000 right off the bat. Terrorists know when they are in a weak negotiating position, whether or not they let on.

Do: Always start low, settle in the middle.

Do: Be willing to walk away if the numbers aren't right.

Do: Offer Grandma as a trade-in; ask a lot for her, at first.

Don't: Become emotional.

Don't: Become confrontational.

Don't: Act too interested.

Do: Try to find a solution where both parties win.

Do: Let them believe the final decision doesn't rest with you.

For example:

You: I like you, I'm on your side. Let me go talk to my wife and see what she can do.

Terrorist: OK.

You: (leave, talk to wife, return) Well, I tried to talk to her but she just won't go a penny over $250,000.

You should also know and anticipate various tactics that the terrorist may employ in trying to negotiate you up to a higher price. Look out for these classic terrorist negotiation one-liners, and don't be thrown by them:

Terrorist: You're stealing food from my children! I have six hungry kids in Islamabad. You're breaking my balls here.

Terrorist: This deal is only good today. I can't promise you will get this excellent price tomorrow.

Terrorist: I like you. I'm on your side. Hold on, let me talk to my manager and see what he can do.

Terrorist: We'll clean him up, throw in a haircut.

Also watch out for extra charges at the end of the transaction: does the bottom line suddenly appear much larger on the final invoice due to things like a convenience fee, feeding and maintenance charge, and *jihad* and deliverance fee?

You: What the hell is the *jihad* fee?

Terrorist: It comes with everything, sir.

Chapter 7

Tips for Teens: What to Do If Your Teen Gets Invited to Participate in a Terrorist Attack and All the Cool Kids Are In On It

Remember kids, terrorism is never cool. Even if it seems cool, and everyone who is cool is doing it, it's still not cool. This is the kind of message you need to instill in your children, lest they be swooped up into a terrorist scheme before they've even learned to memorize the pledge of allegiance. High schools are dangerous places these days, full of diversity, gambling, under-age sex, and water gun fights. Nothing like the good old high schools where slow dancing was punishable by expulsion. No, today's kids face all sorts of new challenges that parents need to wise up about. In this chapter we are here to help you raise good, safe, non-terrorist children. Let's start with a couple of examples of sticky situations your child might find himself in, and great ideas for how to get himself out! Like this one:

Your son Danny's best friend Kevin just got a new car. Cool! Danny is almost as excited as Kevin. Kevin's coming over to take Danny out for a spin around town after supper. But what happens if . . .

Kevin: Hey Danny, check out the new wheels. You ready to go take a spin around town? Maybe get some sodas down at the cafe?

Danny: Wowee Kevin, that sure is a shiny car. We're gonna get so much ass riding around in this thing.

Kevin: I'll say. But wait, first I got a couple errands to run. I gotta drop my sister's roller skates off at the repair shop, and then swing by Earl's and pick up some weapons-grade anthrax to mail to random congressmen, that's OK, right?

What should Danny do? In this all too familiar scenario, Danny has some major decisions to make. Should he go with Kevin, on the assumption that taking a spin in the new car will land him some major tail, even if it means being an accomplice in a terrorist plot? Or should he stay home, cook a microwave pizza, and masturbate to the pictures in last year's high-school yearbook? Let's help Danny find a way out of this tough situation without coming across like a square. Hey Danny, try some of these:

Danny: Hey Kevin, look, I really would like to go with you, but I just can't get myself involved in a terrorist scheme like this. Maybe you can come by later, after you pick up the anthrax and mail it to random congressmen.

Kevin: Sure, that'd be OK, I guess. I'll pick you up at eight then!

See how easy that was? And Kevin understood completely.

Or:

Danny: Sorry Kev, but I've been allergic to anthrax ever since I was a little boy. It causes me to lose control of my left arm, right leg, and tongue, and it makes my eyes itch. But if you want, we can go throw bags of shit at the old folks home, shoot paintball guns at people on bikes, or drop shopping carts onto the highway.

In this option, Danny was able to maintain his cool, edgy image without getting involved in a dangerous terrorist attack. Way to go Danny!

Let's skip over and see what's happening with Margaret, who's having a blast at her junior year after-prom party. Things are going great, she's got a handsome date who has treated her with the dignity and respect deserved by a queen. But when her date slips away to go hit a beer bong in the bathroom with his friends, and then chase the beer bong with several consecutive triple shots of some liquor so strong that if Margaret even sniffed it she would have a hangover till Homecoming, Margaret is put in a tight situation.

Three people present Margaret with potentially dangerous offers. One person asks Margaret if she would like to go upstairs and smoke a marijuana joint with some school buddies. Another person asks Margaret if she would like to go downstairs

Margaret's Offers

and help assemble a small dirty bomb. And a third person asks Margaret if she would like to go into the pool where several football players and cheerleaders are swimming and having unprotected sex, switching back and forth from one to another in a drunken blur that most of them won't even remember.

Wow, what a tough situation!!!

Lucky for Margaret, we (and you) are here to help her out. Fortunately, since these offers were presented simultaneously, Margaret is in the unique position of being able to use one offer as an excuse to get out of the other offers, without hurting anyone's feelings. We here at *The Ultimate Counterterrorist Home Companion* have a zero terrorism policy, thus we would immediately recommend that Margaret decline the offer to go downstairs and assemble the dirty bomb. As for going upstairs and smoking the marijuana joint, well, it could be worse. At least the other kids will think she is cool and might even stop kicking her when she walks through the school cafeteria. Anyway, it's just a marijuana joint. Stop being such a baby, Margaret!

Now she can politely excuse herself from the person inviting her to go downstairs, by saying she would love to, but she has to go upstairs and smoke a joint. See how easy that was? But wait, what about the pool? That could be dangerous, right? In this case, probably not, in fact. Most pools have chlorine, and chlorine kills most STDs and makes it a lot less likely to get pregnant. Moreover, Margaret is a great swimmer, and nobody's going to remember it anyways, right? Plus, it's prom night, and she'll want to have stories to tell her friends the next day. So we recommend to Margaret that she first go smoke the joint upstairs, then go to the pool and hopefully the football players will still be having unprotected sex. Good luck, Margaret, and take some pictures!

In our next scenario, our hero Greg is walking past the girl he has had a crush on since ninth grade in the hallway, when he overhears her talking with a friend about an explosive device that they are building in the abandoned chemistry lab under the gym with which they intend to blow up the Sears Tower. Greg is a good American and feels torn between the woman he loves and his country. How can Greg make sure the explosive device doesn't get to the Sears Tower and protect the woman he loves? (Who ironically thinks he is a total creep and would never go out with him anyway, even if he paid her $1,000, which he has offered to do in the past with no luck. It's not because Greg is bad looking, he just makes silly mistakes, like following her around and taking pictures of her through her window at home.)

It's not so hard—get creative, Greg! Why not tell your school counselor about the explosive device in the chemistry lab, but say you heard someone else talking about it. Like, for example . . . Earl. People will believe you because he is different, and plus, he was involved in the whole anthrax scheme with Kevin, so he had it coming to him. Now Greg has stopped the terrorist plot, and he doesn't have to take down all the pictures of that girl that he has on his wall.

Sure, it all seems very easy if your teenager would just take the time to read this guide, but we have to keep in mind that most teenagers consider reading to be about as enjoyable as dentistry prior to the advent of anesthesia. Or maybe being eaten by a lion. Either way, it may be difficult to convince your teenager to read this chapter. So it's up to you as a parent to lead by example, and show your teenager that there are lots of ways to be cool that don't involve terrorism. Try to remember some of the things that made someone cool back in the good old days. What happened to drag racing? That was pretty cool. How about joining a gang? Gang fights are always cool. And what about doing psychedelic drugs at lunchtime? That's gotta be cool still. So spend quality time with your teenagers, help them get access to things like souped-up cars and psychedelic drugs—if you do, they'll be a lot less likely to turn to terrorism for self-esteem.

A Note On Drugs

Fun Fact: *82% of opium-based drugs in the United States come from terrorist-friendly nations. Money spent on heroin and heroin-related drugs ends up helping to fund terrorism.*

Q: What can I do to help without becoming a total loser?

A: Instead of heroin, which comes from Afghanistan, how about trying cocaine, which comes from Latin American countries like Colombia? Plus, cocaine is more social and not damaging to your health. And you don't lose your teeth and get needle marks up and down your arm.

Q: Do cool people do cocaine?

A: Alleged users include Paris Hilton, Nicole Richie, the Olsen Twins, Lindsay Lohan, Snoop Dog, Courtney Love . . .

Q: Isn't it possible that Paris Hilton would still be my friend one day even if I don't do coke with her?

A: Yeah, good luck with that.

Q: Specifically, where can I get cocaine?

A: See that minority guy on the corner, looking up and down the block for police officers? If he doesn't know, he'll be able to direct you to someone who does.

Q: Are you sure this stuff is good for my health?

A: Definitely.

Q: What other drugs do you recommend that don't come from Afghanistan?

A: All non-opiate-based narcotics, like methamphetamines, acid, mescaline, psilocybin, glue (authors' choice), OxyContin, PCP, AMT, alcohol, barbiturates, Valium, and large doses of Robitussin.

Chapter 8

Securing Your Home: Booby Traps, Land Mines, and Strategic Mail-Opening Strategies

Right now, your home is an open invitation to terrorists. You might as well hang a flashing neon sign outside saying, "Terrorists Welcome! Please Leave Bombs and Chemical Weapons in the Hallway." So clearly, you need to do something about it, and soon.

Let's start with your front lawn. You've probably spread enough highly toxic weed killer out there to nurture a lovely, green monoculture, while ensuring the life-choking runoff finds its way to our increasingly polluted oceans, but when was the last time you sowed a mine field? Can't remember? Then most likely the answer is "Never." Which means you're *way* overdue.

But don't just rush to your computer, get on eBay, and buy a bunch of land mines. You have to *plan*. Where are the best spots to plant a mine? Which are the most effective models? For example, if you really want to "send a message" to the Terrorist Community, it might be better to choose a model more apt to maim than to kill. Most important: *make a map of your mine field.*

Mine Field

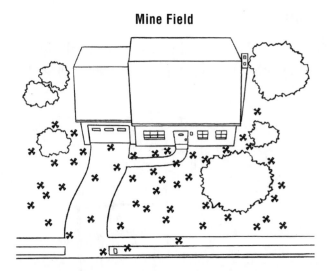

If you can't remember where you've put them, they're going to be less of a help and more of a nuisance. And make sure your family, and a few, carefully selected friends, know where they are.

Before long, your home will be the envy of your neighbors, and will strike fear in the hearts of terrorists, mail carriers, meter readers, and cable guys alike.

You should also secure your doors and windows.

Unsafe Door

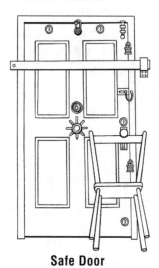

Safe Door

Mail Policy

The best and safest mail policy is one of abstinence only. We strongly recommend you place the following sign next to your mailbox:

In the event that you continue to receive mail despite your clearly marked sign, you will want to have an idea of what is suspicious mail and what is not. For many people, making this distinction can be difficult. Luckily, we have helpful sources like this book and FEMA. Here are some actual tips from www.FEMA.gov/areyouready/, which are there to help you recognize which packages are suspicious and which are not. They describe some signs of suspicious packages including those which:

— "Have protruding wires or aluminum foil, strange odors, or stains."

— "Have excessive postage or packaging material."

— "Have misspellings of common words."

— "Are lopsided or oddly shaped."

And most important in our opinion:
— "Are marked with threatening language."

Q: But how do I know what is Threatening and what is Not Threatening Language?

A: Great question. Here are some examples:

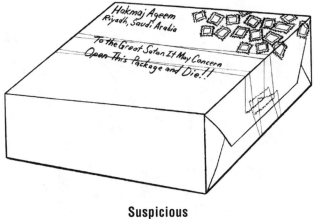

Suspicious

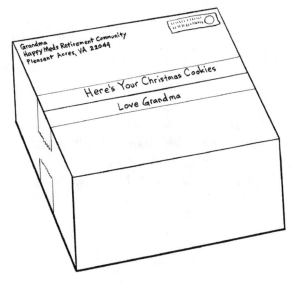

Less Suspicious

Remodeling

You'll also want to consider incorporating the following into any remodeling you do to make your home terrorist-ready:

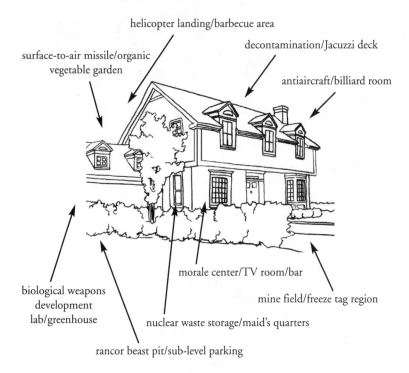

helicopter landing/barbecue area

decontamination/Jacuzzi deck

surface-to-air missile/organic vegetable garden

antiaircraft/billiard room

morale center/TV room/bar

biological weapons development lab/greenhouse

mine field/freeze tag region

nuclear waste storage/maid's quarters

rancor beast pit/sub-level parking

But if the terrorists get access to the preceding blueprints, you're in even more trouble than you were before. So when this chapter ends, dispose of it properly.

This chapter has now ended. Please rip out this page and eat it.

Chapter 9

Moats:
How to Make Them,
Are They Still Useful?

Building a moat is not as simple as most people think: make
your children dig all day long for eight months and wait for
rain. No. In fact there are a lot of important things to consider
before you begin building your moat. Should this moat contain
alligators? What happens if the alligators somehow get out of
the moat and into your home or that of a neighbor? What really
is the difference between an alligator and a crocodile, because
they really are basically the same thing, right? Is moat building
against your particular city's construction code? Is having a
crocodile or alligator against your particular city's wildlife
regulation statutes? Will my drawbridge be sturdy enough to
support the weight of my large but not overly indulgent six-
wheel SUV? What's the best way for my child to fight off an
alligator if it already has one of his/her limbs in its jaws?

Yes. Before you begin the process of isolating yourself from
society completely, you will need to read this chapter.

Q: How wide does my moat have to be?

A: Let's be reasonable here: an average, physically fit adult
human cannot pole-vault a water barrier of more than 15 feet.
So there's no reason to get hysterical and build a 30-foot moat.

Q: How deep should my moat be?

A: Use your own judgment, but it should be at least deep enough so you only have to fill it up three-quarters of the way, making it more difficult for the alligators to escape. Again, your common sense is your best guide.

Q: What about the situation when the alligator has escaped and is in my living room?

A: Wave your arms while jumping up and down and shouting, making yourself look as large and intimidating as possible. Unless that was for bears. Either way, it's better than doing nothing and being eaten. Special Hint: Do not swim across your moat with an open wound. Alligators are attracted to blood.

If you don't have the necessary resources or land area to build your own moat, there are moated communities, where one moat serves everyone, and moat-maintenance costs are shared. They sometimes offer Jacuzzis and gyms. Also, it's a shrewd real estate investment, since as the rate of terrorism rises, you can expect the value of a home in a moated community to increase. (A silver lining to the cloud.) But what is a moat really? In the true, metaphorical sense of the word. Is the Pacific Ocean really just a big, salty moat between our home and that of our Islamic neighbors? And what is this chapter really about at its core? Really, we are talking about water, right? Water and water-based issues. So let's address some of these water issues that are so central to the meaning of this chapter.

Guarding Your Ports

Do you live on a lake or a private beach community? This is kind of like sitting at one of those emergency exit seats on an airplane: it's a lot of added, voluntary responsibility. You have to be extra vigilant in guarding your port for the rest of the inland community. And you have to worry about having some kind of nervous breakdown and opening the door in mid-flight while all the passengers go flying out of the plane.

Invest in a good pair of binoculars. Spend a good portion of your day watching people, especially scantily clad people.

Invest in a patrol jet ski. Yes, they're expensive, but it's your duty.

Don't be too alarmed. Despite all the talk from pundits and politicians, our terrorist-movie-based research indicates that port attacks are not terrorists' method of choice. They prefer the more exciting skydiving/helicopter/snowboarding-type attacks. What could be more boring for a terrorist than launching an attack by a slow-moving container ship!?

Q: So what are you saying? Guard my port or don't guard my port?

A: Yes. Now it is time to move on to the next section. But first, let's check in with Jibby and Koko on the following page.

Kidz Korner

Counterterrorist Crossword Puzzle

Give this crossword puzzle a try. We've filled in a few letters to make it easier so you don't have to think so hard!

Jibby　　Koko

DOWN
1 Questioning the war ＿＿ the troops.
2 When you criticize the President you ＿＿＿ the terrorists.
3 We're fighting them over there so we don't have to ＿＿＿ them here.

ACROSS
4 Democrats' only idea for the war on terror.
5 ＿＿＿ are not trustworthy to make important decisions on national security.

Answers:

The History of Terrorism and What Your Government Is Doing to Stop It

Chapter 10

A History of the World Before 9/11: All in All, a Pretty Smooth Ride

When life first emerged on this planet, some 6,000 years ago, life was simple and pure. People lived in small villages and tribes, where the men would hunt the inferior species and bring home carcasses for their wives to cook. Everyone was happy. Even the hunted animals were happy to serve a purpose in such a harmonious system. The children would work with their mothers to create products made of beads mostly (fig. 1) as well as

Fig. 1. Beads

woven baskets (fig. 2) in which important tribal items could be transported.

These woven baskets and beaded goods could then be traded for sheep (fig. 3) and oxen, which would in turn produce eggs and milk

Fig. 2. Woven basket

that could be eaten as side dishes, accompanying the savory meat from the freshly killed village animals. People would build campfires and sing primitive songs in rounds while dancing around the fire like

Fig. 3. Sheep

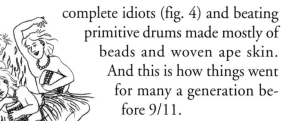

Fig. 4. Primitive People

complete idiots (fig. 4) and beating primitive drums made mostly of beads and woven ape skin. And this is how things went for many a generation before 9/11.

Unfortunately, due to the limited number of people, and ignorance of basic gene theory, brothers would marry sisters, cousins marry uncles and so forth, which produced people like the bad guys in *Deliverance*, and even more unfortunately, different races. With the emergence of different races came the idea of different languages and religions, which really started to confuse the whole deal and led to a significant amount of yelling and basketball games ending in fist fights due to miscommunication and intentional fouling (fig. 5).

It was during this time that "history" happened, a lot of it in a place called "Europe" (fig. 6), which was really boring, except for the knights (who actually worked mostly days), who existed in the Dark Ages, which sounds a lot cooler than it was.

There was also some history that happened even

Fig. 5. Basketball

farther away, in places like China, but nobody really knows about that.

Luckily, with the invention of boats we soon discovered America, an uninhabited land where we could start again and learn from our mistakes. In America, people could live (remembering this time to only make children with distant neighbors), and leave the other races to live separately, in hotter, less excellent countries which consisted mostly of sand (fig. 7) and large biting insects. Meanwhile, we Americans lived for many more generations in complete peace until the advent of television, which allowed the people in the hot, sandy countries to see what an excellent country we had found. Sick and tired of the itchy and at times painful insect bites, jealous of our prosperity, and driven to the point of insanity with sexual desire for our movie stars, specifically Angelina Jolie, the other races came up with a new invention, one that would change the scope of history forever: Terrorism.

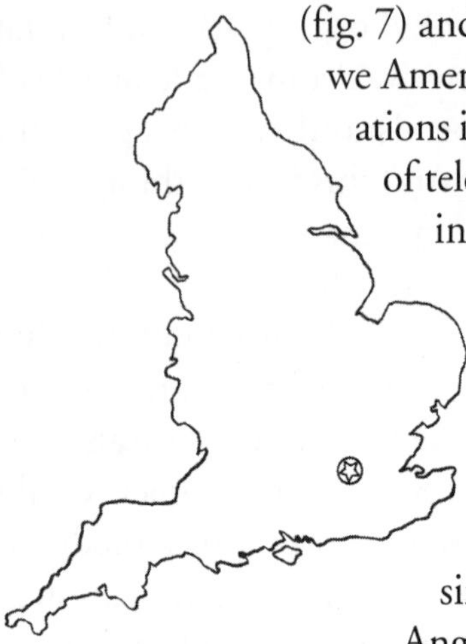

Fig. 6. Europe

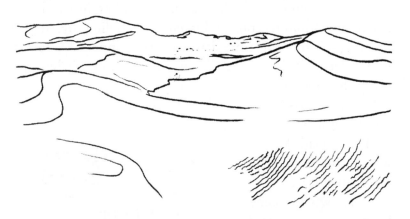

Fig. 7. Sand

Chapter 11

A History of the World After 9/11: Evil Makes Its Entrance

Through terrorism, the other races could express their frustration and confusion and passionate desire for Angelina Jolie in a way that would be remembered almost as much as an action scene from *Mr. and Mrs. Smith* or *Tomb Raider*. Only the devastating effect terrorism would have would be much greater than even *Mr. and Mrs. Smith* and *Tomb Raider* put together. It was even worse than having to watch both of those movies back to back eight times in a row, because after a terrorist attack, people were left injured and dead, unlike after watching those movies, where at worst a person might suffer mild headaches and various episodes of projectile vomiting. Terrorism was in fact so much worse than even the worst Angelina Jolie movies that it made us create an entire new bureaucracy in our government with a brand-new task: protecting America.

Americans began to realize that the peace and prosperity we had come to take for granted was in jeopardy. The other races could no longer be ignored. In a blur of patriotic panic, we began to study the people outside of our borders: where they live, how their language works, how to cook without microwaves. And what we discovered was terrifying. The people living in these countries where terrorism was invented were more than just angry and batshit insane about Angelina Jolie . . . they were evil. And there's really not a lot of negotiating with Evil. So Americans united, stood hand in hand, and took up arms in what we had always feared might happen, our first War.

Q: Why is the history after 9/11 chapter so much shorter than the history before 9/11 chapter?

A: When we went to print, the history of the world before 9/11 was considerably longer than the history of the world after 9/11, specifically 1,000 times longer.

Q: How come there are no illustrations in this chapter?

A: After 9/11 art is no longer a relevant concept. The world has become a much too serious place for acrylics, crayons, and watercolors. Which brings us, conveniently, to our next chapter.

Q: I liked the one with the pictures better.

A: Your negativity has just destroyed a perfect segue.

Chapter 12

No-Longer-Relevant Concepts: Civil Liberties, the Multi-Party System, Karaoke

In this chapter we look at how the world will be different in the post-9/11 environment. Knowing what we now know about the world, we have to part with some of our early, naive ideas about what is good policy, what is good culture, and develop a more mature view of how the world should function.

You see, the growth of a nation is like the growth of a person in many ways. It starts out screaming and covered in blood, eventually learns to use a toilet, suffers periods of rapid growth accompanied by limited limb control, acne, and desperate attempts to get other people (nations) to take off their clothes, and eventually ends up old, tired, and thoroughly convinced that the retirement community staff are stealing its sweaters at night to trade for weapons with the North Koreans. 9/11 hit somewhere between potty training and getting your ass kicked by the older kids freshman year of high school. At this critical juncture in our nation's growth, we must learn to exchange our childlike interests in flying superheroes, Santa Claus, and the Constitution for more practical and useful interests like learning how not to get your ass kicked by tenth graders, rendition, and wiretapping.

Our Constitution was written by a bunch of guys wearing funny-looking wigs who had nothing more to fear than the British Navy, which was just a bunch of other guys in funny-looking wigs in big sailboats! No wonder the document they produced was quaint and naive! They lived in quaint, naive times.

In the editing process of a script, we in the movie business, and by we, we mean other people, use terms like "cut" and "save" to describe material that they are going to "cut" and "save." So basically what is being said is that in the post-9/11 movie script, the Constitution is an obvious "cut." Civil liberties, well that goes with the Constitution (you can't cut the sex scene but keep the naked boobs). The multi-party system? That was starting to get confusing even before 9/11, and, well, boobs again, same reason. Karaoke? While not specifically mentioned in the Constitution, karaoke obviously should never have happened in the first place. But what other things should be "cut" from the script? Or if you prefer the previous metaphor: Let's take a look at some of the other concepts that we as a nation must rapidly "grow beyond" if we are to survive the "middle school" era of our maturation.

 Sensible foreign policies

 Birkenstocks

 Habeas corpus

 Bubble wrap

 The whole fascination with π

 Movies starring Adam Sandler

 Foreign languages

The whole fascination with pies

 Public education

 The letter Q

 Movies where reality turns out to be a digital illusion

 Movies where the main characters turn out to be the same person

 The United Nations

Semicolons

Q: Why does the trash can guy gotta be black?

A: If he was white, you wouldn't be able to see him, because the background is white. And who's ever heard of a green trash man?

We've made a lot of progress on some of this, but there's still a lot left to do. But don't feel overwhelmed. We've already cut out so much constitutional fat on our post-9/11 diet that admiring nations around the world stop us on the street to comment, "*Mon Dieu*, you look great! Have you lost weight?"

We must keep in mind that as uncomfortable and unattractive as the acne of this adolescent, transitional period (the War in Iraq) is, it will soon be nothing more than a dermatological scar in our history books. We will be a stronger people and nation as adults. Which brings us, conveniently, to our next chapter.

Chapter 13

Invading Iraq: It's the Thought That Counts

So what has our government been doing to help out in the fight? The 2003 invasion of Iraq (fig. 1) was a brilliant move in our government's efforts to combat terrorism, filled with subtleties that are not often noticed by radical left wing organizations like CNN. Invading Iraq is the equivalent of avoiding a bar fight by pouring a milkshake on your head. Just when your enemy is so angry that he is ready to punch you in the head, you do something so unexpected and bizarre as to make your enemy reconsider his plan of action, reconsider his assessment of you as a threat, and even go home and rethink the whole direction of his life. You've avoided confrontation and disarmed your enemy, at the mere cost of a little embarrassing milkshake on your head in front of your friends, the bartender, and the United Nations. Your enemies now know that your reactions will be so irrational and unpredictable that they will give up trying to anticipate them, realizing that at any moment, you could do just about

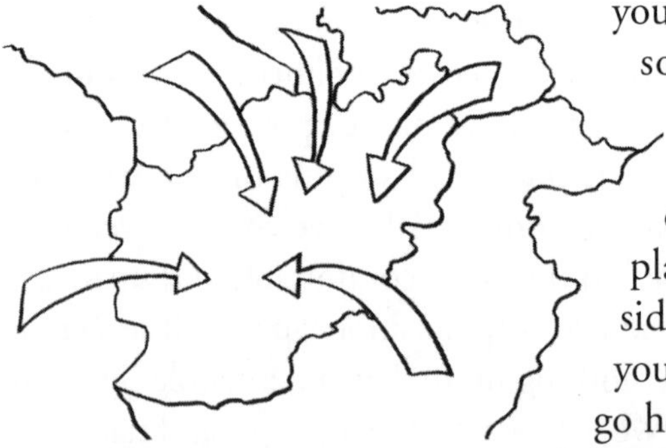

Fig. 1. Iraq

anything for almost any reason at all. This is the most intimidating type of foreign policy, and the most intimidating way to handle a milkshake.

People just don't like to mess with insane people. For example, consider how we all enjoy kicking, harassing, and throwing things at homeless people every now and then, but we all routinely avoid the homeless person who stands on the corner yelling loudly about how the Vietnamese government is putting chemicals in his water to prep his body for effective testing when the aliens come back after next year's Super Bowl. We sort of walk to the other side of the road when we see that homeless guy, without even a snide remark.

The invasion of Iraq was just like throwing a wild pitch every now and then to keep the batter guessing, and you know what? It worked. Our enemies and friends alike no longer consider us capable of rational thought, and that, friends, is right where we want them. And best of all, just like in the Milkshake Scenario, nobody got hurt. Actually, maybe that's not such a good metaphor. In the chapters to come, we will continue our search for a more appropriate metaphor explaining the importance of the Iraq war to people who get a little too much of their information from CNN.

Q: What if there is another terrorist attack? Suppose someone does slip past our unguarded posts?

A: Don't worry, there's plenty of other countries to invade, how about South America?
1) It's close.
2) It's not too far away.
3) Nice beaches
4) The language is similar, most words are very close in
    sound. For example:

            English: cat   Spanish: cato
            English: chair   Spanish: chairo

Q: How do you say, "Let's move on to the next chapter" in Spanish?

A: "Let move on to el next chaptero." But first, let's see what Koko and Jibby are up to!

Kidz Korner

What's Wrong with This Picture?

There are exactly five things wrong with this picture. Can you find them?

Jibby   **Koko**

Answers: 1) Upside-down picture 2) Fish out of water 3) Stripes on flag going wrong way 4) Too many fingers on Lynndie England's hand 5) She isn't an ice skater

Chapter 14

The Color-Coded Terror Alert System: Giving Citizens an Exact, Rainbowy Gauge of How Fearful to Be at Any Given Moment

Not so very long ago, in the good times before the War on Terror, we knew everything we needed to know about the day ahead simply by checking the time, the weather, and the Photo of the Day on www.Nakedcelebrities.com.

What we *didn't* know was exactly how fearful we should be. But now, thanks to our government, we have an accurate, daily, color-coded chart. Today we can access the precise, government-approved fear level (updated every 10 minutes), while simultaneously checking out www.Nakedcelebrities.com. No other country in the world has a system like this.

Q: If the government is anticipating and planning to disrupt a terrorist plot, why would they make this information available to everyone, including the terrorists, thus giving them ample opportunity to reschedule the attack on a day when the Alert Level is lower?

A: Although this policy has many logical flaws, your government has never been good at lying, and feels obliged to keep the public informed about everything they know at all times. You can fault the policy but must respect the remarkable display of integrity. When was the last time you were completely honest with *anybody?*

Q: Me personally?

A: No, not you. A general, hypothetical reader.

In case you're unfamiliar with the chart, we've copied it from the DHS website and pasted it here:

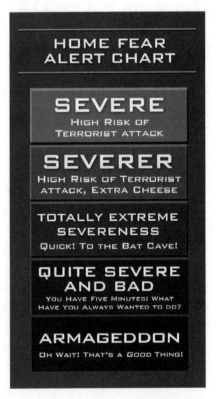

This chart is brought to you by Brown Fizzy Cola
It's Never Too Late to Enjoy the Refreshing Taste of Fizzy!

Q: Why isn't this in color?

A: It *is* in color. There must be something wrong with your copy. You should buy another one.

There are many nuances clandestinely embedded in the Fear Chart through subtle differences in shading. These secret, coded messages were originally intended for government employees only! But by squinting real hard at the green, or lowest alert level, you'll be able to determine if your fear sub-level should be Complacent, when goofing off and telling knock-knock jokes is recommended, or Oblivious, when you can totally ignore unattended packages in public places that emit ticking noises. You'll also find out which shade of orange means Go to Your Underground Bomb Shelter Now, and which means Heightened Danger, Sylvester Stallone Is About to Make Another *Rocky* Sequel.

If you live in a sparsely populated area, like maybe Western Montana (fig. 1), you might be wondering if your level of panic should be the same as the panic level for your cousin Bruce, who moved to New York City the day he graduated from high school and who recently landed a small part in an equity-waiver production of *Hamlet,* according to the FBI Joint Terrorism Task Force, which just happens to know.

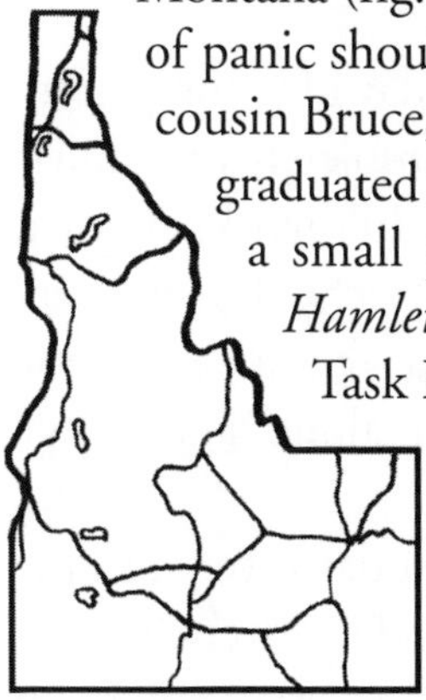

The answer is that you and Bruce have exactly the same panic level, a fact recognized by Congress when they slashed the federal funding for homeland security for big states like New York and raised them for little states like Montana.

Fig. 1.
Western Montana

And if you're wondering why they did that, it's because Montana has exactly the same number of United States senators as New York.

By the way, congratulations, Bruce!

Chapter 15

Making New Friends throughout the World: Kidnapping, Secret Detention, and Torture

Another thing your government is doing is making new friends and allies throughout the world. Making new friends can be difficult.

We all remember that frightening first day of kindergarten, when we had to face a classroom full of completely unfamiliar faces. Somehow, it seemed, all the other children knew each other—maybe they'd gone to the same preschool or were all members of the same family or had been at the same juvenile detention facility together. But we were all alone in a strange world. How to make friends?

The dilemma we found ourselves in that day is very like the dilemma the United States finds itself in today. After all, we're a relatively young country compared to all those countries in Europe and around the world, who all seem to know each other and speak each other's languages and have exclusive little clubs and cliques, designed, it seems, just to exclude us, to make us feel like an "outsider," to keep us from ever getting a turn on the "seesaw." So what do we do to make friends in this forbidding environment? We do exactly what we did that first day in kindergarten: we march right up to the first little country we see, and punch them in the face!

Yes, the same methods we used to "break the ice" with our classmates that day are still valid in the field of international relations. We showed those little bastards in kindergarten that they couldn't just exclude us from the fun, and as a result we made lots and lots of friends, or at least the other children were afraid of us and hated us, which is pretty much the same thing. There are also other techniques we can use in our foreign policy and military campaigns to win friends and influence people all around the globe in the same ways we did in kindergarten. For example:

Preemptive War

Exercising Our Responsibilities as the World's Only Remaining Superpower

During Arts and Crafts, in the same way we tasted the paste even though all the "adults" told us not to, we as a nation have "tasted" and found "quite delicious" all sorts of things the older nations advised against.

When we had play dates with other children and we would only play the games we wanted to play and change the rules to make sure we always won, eventually they wouldn't have play dates with us anymore. So we bombed their country.

There's also the fine art of keeping old friends we made in kindergarten. Sometimes sending a biannual e-mail is enough.

But are your core values still the same? Maybe you've moved on with your life, developed new interests and relationships, but they're still stuck on habeas corpus.

Then there are the early childhood friends that you realize were not really that great to begin with, even though they were very supportive during that emotional break-up. They gave you a nice statue, which seemed very thoughtful at the time, but has now turned green, and is really just taking up valuable desk space. You realize they're not worth the e-mail, and you might consider boycotting their wines.

Q: What if your friends no longer like extended metaphors and just want you to move on to the next chapter?

A: Those people were never your friends.

Q: I was really looking forward to hearing more in this chapter about kidnapping, secret detention, and torture.

A: We tried to deal with the subjects delicately by turning them all into a kindergarten metaphor, so we really have dealt with them, just in a lighthearted way.

Q: Yeah, but specifically, I want to hear more about torture.

A: We must have gone to different kindergartens.

SPECIAL ALERT!

Creating a Shadow Family: Important Note Just for Dad

Creating a Shadow Family is a responsibility for Dad. The Shadow Family must live in another neighborhood/city and center around a Back-up Wife in case the Primary Family is destroyed. This will ensure Continuity of Family.

Your Back-up Wife should be younger, probably; also very beautiful and sexually attractive. It took 6,000 years of selective reproduction to produce Brangelina, let's not start all over again.

It's important that your Primary Wife not know about the Shadow Family so in the event that she is captured, she can't possibly reveal the location of the Shadow Family. Also, the Shadow Family must never call, under any circumstances, the Primary Family.

It's a good idea to have Shadow Golf Clubs in case your Primary Golf Clubs are destroyed by terrorists.

If possible, names for your Shadow Family should be the same or similar to those of the Primary Family to avoid the awkward situation when you say, "I love you, Karen," and Primary Wife responds, "It's Meg."

You should have a Shadow Nanny so there's somebody to care for the Shadow Children when you're off at your Shadow Bar with your Shadow Buddies.

Also, for canine ev-olutionary purposes, your

Shadow Dog　　　**Primary Dog**

Shadow Dog should be smart, whereas your Primary Dog just needs to be lovable.

Advanced Option: Shadow Shadow Wife.

Q: If Primary Wife finds out about Shadow Wife, will she understand?

A: Monogamy is a pre-9/11 mentality. She will probably understand.

Chapter 16

Avoiding God's Wrath by Banning Gay Marriage

"What," you may be thinking, "could gay marriage possibly have to do with terrorism?" A legitimate question, which demands a serious answer. But first we have to answer another legitimate question, which is what, exactly, is God's position on gay marriage?

Many moral cowards shrink from characterizing God's exact position on the hot-button political issues of the day, but thankfully there are experts on God's opinions, especially in the Evangelical movement, who can fill us in. According to these experts, God created homosexuals in a moment of absentmindedness, and only later realized what a horrible mistake He had made. But it was too late to do anything about it, because like poison ivy and reality television shows, they already existed, and He has some kind of rule that He can't take back anything He did, even if it turned out badly. But that doesn't mean He wants them to make a deep, long-term commitment like marriage, vowing to remain together in sickness and in health, for richer or poorer, forsaking all others until death do them part, and then violate those oaths and get divorced and remarried and violate their oaths again like normal heterosexuals.

He intends something entirely different for them, and it involves bathhouses and other stuff normal people don't want to even think about, which we will examine and illustrate in this chapter. (Just kidding!)

The point is you want to stay on God's good side as a general strategy for the War on Terrorism. Since God hasn't spoken to you personally since the last time you dropped acid, you have to listen carefully to those in regular dialogue with Him. What is God blogging about today? (And by "today" we mean this epoch, and by "blogging" we mean posting angry rants on the Internet, while wearing pajamas and eating frozen pizzas.) Fortunately, we keep up with His Holy Website. Here is God's latest post:

3:02 A.M.
Current mood: Cranky
Currently listening to: OutKast: *Stankonia*
Stem cells! Who do these scientists think they are? When I create a life, it's not theirs to put in a petri dish and play around with! I might just have to send some Terror down to America!

COMMENTS (409 million, not all included)

By: Backstreetgirl-25 at 3:03 A.M.
Absolutely! Clear-headed, well stated! Thanx! You've come through again with another great one. By the way, God, you probably already know, but my daughter Jennifer is applying for college, and we could really use Your help. She didn't do that well on her SATs.

By: Handyman007 at 3:03 A.M.
You are missing the point, as usual. We've all heard deities using this line of argument. It wasn't convincing then, it isn't convincing now. At least come up with something original.

This concludes Section Two of the book. Feel free to get up, stretch, walk around, maybe make some popcorn. Or you can check in with Jibby and Koko!

Jibby   **Koko**

Kidz Korner

Anagrams

Can you help Jibby and Koko match these important counterterrorist key phrases with their corresponding anagrams? (An anagram is the rearrangement of the letters of a word or phrase to form other words or phases that hopefully include words like "butt.") The first two we've already done for you so you'll get the idea, because we know things like this are hard for you.)

Stay the Course
Ass Erect Youth

Patriot Act
Taco Rat Pit

Counterterrorist Phrase Anagram

Plan for Victory   Warts Nerd Pie

Temporary Surge   Anus Cleanup Row

War President   Gay Serum Report

Nucular Weapons   Crap of Vinyl Rot

A Bunch of Chapters We Decided to Put in Section Three

Chapter 17

For Parents: A Special Chapter Just for You

Chores and Punishments in a Post-9/11 World

In the same way chain gangs were a positive advancement in punishment and rehabilitation, you too can add a productive quality to the correctional department of your own family. Dunce caps and "Go to Your Room" add no capital gain to your net family worth. Feeding, walking, or bathing detainees, on the other hand, provides a learning experience about responsibility, as well as taking care of chores that have to be done by someone. If they can't handle the responsibility of walking a detainee, they're not ready for a dog.

In a post-9/11 world, certain chores can now be considered punishments. For example, opening mail. It is only common sense to select one family member to be Primary Mail Opener. This could be looked at as merely a chore or, more accurately, a punishment. Suggested dialogue:

You: Samuel Edward Stephens, get over here right now.

Your Child: Aw, Mom.

You: Did I hear you use the "s" word in front of Grandma?

Your Child: Socialist?

You: No.

Your Child: Social Security?

You: No. "Shit." You just earned yourself Primary Mail Opener duty for a week, mister.

Your Child: Aw, Mom.

Similarly, taking out the garbage, once just a chore, is now also a punishment due to the backyard mine field. It's also a Teaching Moment—your child will have to learn where the mines are placed. Studies have shown nine out of ten children will learn this way, like throwing a baby in a pool.

Once you start thinking like this, there's no limit to the number of everyday chores that can be incorporated into your disciplinary program. Be creative!

What to Do When Your Son Tells You He Wants to Change His Name to Habib and Move to Afghanistan

Maybe you didn't notice when your son grew a beard and insisted that his bed face Mecca. You figured that was a phase most teenagers go through. Maybe you looked the other way when he took down the posters of Kobe Bryant dunking on Shaquille O'Neal, and put up posters of Sheik Omar Abdel-Rahman dunking on Muqtada al-Sadr. That was just healthy teenage hero worship. But when he bought his ticket to Kabul on your credit card, you could ignore it no longer.

What do you do? You do exactly what you did when your other son tried to become gay: you beat the shit of him, take away his cell phone, and put him into three weeks of intensive counseling at an undisclosed Arizona treatment center. At least this time, it's not so bad. He didn't dishonor the family name.

What to Do If Your Daughter's Cult Leader Decides They Will Be Locking Themselves in a Well-Armed House until Armageddon Next Thursday after Lunch

At least she didn't marry that Jew.

Chapter 18

Are There Terrorists in Your Own Family? No? Are You Sure?

Are You a Terrorist?

Before you can determine whether there are terrorists in your family, you will want to know if you yourself are a terrorist. Maybe you are and do not know. Many terrorists would not consider themselves terrorists even though they are. For example, people who are idiots often do not know they are idiots even though it's quite clear to everyone else. There are very few people who would describe themselves as "not very intelligent, kind of stupid," yet as we know, "not very intelligent, kind of stupid" people are very common. So basically you cannot know if you are intelligent, nor can you know if you are a terrorist.

You personally are probably not a moron because you bought this book, which is a sign of intelligence. Unless someone bought it for you, which means that person who purchased the book is intelligent but you are not necessarily so. Either way, whether or not you are a terrorist is no more or less clear. Here are a few tests to help you determine your terrorist/non-terrorist status.

Please begin by reading the following statements and indicating whether you definitely agree, somewhat agree, somewhat disagree, or definitely disagree with each statement.

I get very upset when I watch political television shows, and sometimes worry that I have little or no control over my own anger.

A) definitely agree
B) somewhat agree
C) somewhat disagree
D) definitely disagree

I feel happiness when I hear of American military casualties and of idolatrous infidels, traitorous apostates, and turncoat decadent Americans in general being destroyed.

A) definitely agree
B) somewhat agree
C) somewhat disagree
D) definitely disagree

It has always been my belief that the victory of Islam will never take place until a Muslim state is established in the manner of the Prophet in the heart of the Islamic world, specifically in the Levant, Egypt, and the neighboring states of the Peninsula and Iraq.

A) definitely agree
B) somewhat agree
C) somewhat disagree
D) definitely disagree

I hate you, stupid American pig! I want you die!! I kill you! I kill you!

A) definitely agree
B) somewhat agree
C) somewhat disagree
D) definitely disagree

I sometimes feel hungry again only 25–30 minutes after eating a large meal.
  A) definitely agree
  B) somewhat agree
  C) somewhat disagree
  D) definitely disagree

You are the richer if you know the stances of the authentic ulema on rulers in times of *jihad* and the defense of the Muslim holy sites.
  A) definitely agree
  B) somewhat agree
  C) somewhat disagree
  D) definitely disagree

Sometimes I fantasize about meeting George Clooney, and wonder if he is as tall in person as he looks in the movies.
  A) definitely agree
  B) somewhat agree
  C) somewhat disagree
  D) definitely disagree

Many of the most learned ulema of Islam such as Izz Bin Abdul Salam, and Ibn Hajar—may God have mercy on them—were Ashari. And many of the most eminent jihadists, whom the Umma resolved unanimously to praise, such as Nur al-Din Bin Zanki and Salahal-Din al-Ayyubi, were Ashari. The mujahedeen sultans who came after them whom the ulema and the historians lauded, such as Sayf al-Din Qatz, and Muhammad al-Fatih, were Ashari or Matridi. They fell into errors, sins, and heresies.
  A) definitely agree
  B) somewhat agree
  C) somewhat disagree
  D) definitely disagree

Duran Duran is the best band of all time.
   A) definitely agree
   B) somewhat agree
   C) somewhat disagree
   D) definitely disagree

If you find yourself circling definitely agree or somewhat agree more often than the other two options, it's possible that you are a terrorist and do not know it. DO NOT PANIC. This is just a preliminary test. We simply have to recommend that you proceed to the advanced section of this test for further analysis.

Advanced Section of This Test

Please look at the following statements or diagrams and try to decide whether these things seem like "Good Things" or "Bad Things." (Correct answers provided below and upside down.)

A) Good Thing   B) Bad Thing

Answer: B) Bad Thing

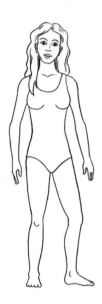

A) Good Thing   B) Bad Thing

Answer: A) Good Thing

Are You a Terrorist? Rorschach Test

Please look at the following image and immediately select the first thing that comes to mind.

A) The Great Satan
B) The time the crusaders came to attack my madrassa
C) A flower

Acceptable Answer: C) A flower

Let's try that again—remember, the first thing that comes to mind.

    A) lovely pieces of shrapnel that could make a great explosive
    B) A shameless woman in public showing her ankles
    C) A man having sex with a horse

Acceptable Answer: C) A man having sex with a horse

Consider the following statement: "There's a geographical area stretching from Spain all the way to Indonesia, in a kind of crescent shape. This could all be one, huge Islamic Empire." I think about this:
    A) Occasionally
    B) All the time
    C) Never

Acceptable answer: C) Never

    If after taking this test you have determined that you are a terrorist, this book is not for you and we would appreciate it if you would give it to someone you know who is not a terrorist. Thanks! :)

Are You a Terrorist? Science Project

Your child is always looking for an easy project for the science fair at the last moment. The question "Are You a Terrorist?" written in bold letters with a Sharpie on a poster board is a good start. Then she could cut out one of those graphics from a newspaper about how to construct an improvised explosive device (IED) or explosively formed penetrator (EFP) and put that on the poster board with all the instructions. Below that, with another color marking pen, she can write the questions: "Why did you read this? Are you really that interested in how to construct a device like this?" and then follow with, "Conclusion: If you read all about this, you probably are a terrorist." This could take up most of the poster board, if properly spaced. Then maybe your child could glue a golf ball on the poster board representing the earth, and maybe a cotton ball for the moon, just to make it look more like a science project. And let's face it, your eight-year-old and her science project aren't exactly going to be advancing the theory of quantum mechanics in any meaningful way, so she might as well be doing something patriotic.

Are There Terrorists in Your Family?

When asked if there are terrorists in your family, you're probably quick to answer, "No way!!" But after a bit of thought, you'll more than likely add, "Except maybe for my brother-in-law . . . and then there's Great Aunt Maud" (fig. 1).

Let's examine what happens when you take a moment to go beyond that first, defensive reaction and consider the question more seriously. You have to keep a close eye on everyone these days, your family especially. What are they up to when you're not around? With what types of friends is your son associating? With what types of women is your husband having affairs? What's that Chinese stuff mean on your daughter's new tattoo? Why

Fig. 1. Great Aunt Maud

did your nephew David change his name to "Abdul-Rami-Khaleem, Warrior of God"? Can you really add a description like that to your name, like "Katherine Davis, Best Mother in Wellville," and insist people call you that?

To keep track of all this stuff, here's a simple checklist you can fill out in the privacy of your own den or bomb shelter:

— Does this person belong to any known subversive groups operating in your area, like so-called "civil rights" organizations or "peace" groups?

— Does this person attend the right church? Regularly?

— Does this person sometimes do things that irritate or annoy you?

— Do you ever feel anxiety or sadness at night?

— Do you ever want more out of life than you're currently getting?

— Have you considered joining the Church of Scientology?

— Have you seen my keys? I could have sworn they were next to the TV.

— Have you ever caught this person getting her news from any of those . . . other . . . cable news stations?

— Does this person always root for the "home team" in sporting events, or does she sometimes root for the "visiting" team? Why?

— Has this person ever been a bit slow to leap up to attention for the singing of "The Spar-Spangled Banner"?

— Does she always sing, and does she know the words?

— Has she ever been overheard to question authority in this setting, like disputing the call of the legally constituted judge, in this case, the umpire?

— Does she order beer and hot dogs, or does she bring vacuum-sealed baked tofu with sesame seeds in a red wine vinaigrette?

— Has she been known to frequent foreign restaurants? (We're not talking about British pubs here, we're talking French, Italian, or—special alert—Middle Eastern places where they lie around on pillows and eat with their hands and other completely disgusting stuff we can't even mention in a family-oriented antiterrorism guide.)

By this point in your Relative Survey, a pattern should be emerging, either a clean bill of health, or a "person of interest" profile.

If it's a "person of interest," it's time to start a casual conversation. But, first things first, you need to break the ice with a pitcher of extra-strength margaritas. It's a delicious concoction, and they won't really know what's hit 'em until they're singing the Mexican national anthem, or maybe "The Internationale." Wait about 15 minutes before you start with your conversational gambits. Here are a few suggestions:

— "I paid $3.22 a gallon for gas today at the Buy'N Save! Can you believe it? Doesn't it make you just want to strap a belt of dynamite on under your cardigan and blow up the local farmers' market?"

— "Won't you try a shish kebab? By the way, do you happen to know what "shish kebab" really means? I've always wondered."

Make a note of just how eagerly your suspect grabs for the Middle Eastern treat. Also recommended: have a heaping bowl of couscous and maybe another of tabouli, and see who goes for it. And for dessert, whip up a tempting *mousse au chocolat.* Now step back and see who dives in.

By this time your target has pieces of greasy, very foreign food dribbling down her chin. Try not to reveal how much this turns your stomach. Remember, the safety and security of your Homeland depends on it. Press your advantage.

Conversational gambits for Mom:
— "I know I'm her mother and I should try to be tolerant, but I just don't understand the music my daughter likes. I really prefer music with sitars don't you (fig. 2)? Something about that wobbly tone that just makes me want to not dance, show any skin, or be seen in public."

— "Last night I felt so useless trying to help my daughter with her geography homework. I could remember the capital of Delaware and Kansas, but I just couldn't remember the capital of Pakistan. Anyone have a clue?"

Fig. 2. Sitar

Note the response carefully. Which means (sorry!) you can only have a sip or two of the margaritas. We don't want to get sloppy here or the next morning when you're trying to record the results—you won't be able to recall these conversations and your notepad will be a soggy mess.

By following these simple but effective instructions, adding creative ideas of your own specific to your individual relatives, you'll have a list of probable terrorists in your family before you can say, "Hello, FBI?"

Freudian Slips

Be keenly aware of any casual slips of the tongue that may reveal the subconscious or secret thoughts of your target family member. The following are "Freudian slips" you should consider suspicious:

— "I'd like some breath mints, a Slurpee, and a Pakistan of cigarettes."
— "Let's go to hiJack in the Box."
— "A double cheeseburger and a suicide order of fries."
— "I'm quite thirsty and planning on destroying your country."

Projection

Speaking of Freud, there is the Freudian concept of projection. Does somebody you know seem to think everyone *else* is a terrorist? It's like that one guy on the football team that goes out of his way to accuse everyone else of being gay and then hangs himself 30 years later when he realizes it was really him the whole time.

There's also psychosocial projections like white Americans saying all Mexicans are lazy, Trekkies accusing all *Star Wars* fans of being weird, and white Americans saying Iraqis don't value human life. Of course, the last one is true, so maybe it's not such a good example.

A: Under the desk, up to the roof, over the rainbow, boxers or briefs is acceptable, and "to go."

Q: *What the bloody hell are you talking about?*

A: We told you that we were going to answer the questions on page 14 at a time when you were not expecting it. By not recognizing this, you've let us down once again.

Chapter 19

Good Morning! Checking for Bombs under Your Car

There's nothing quite like waking up in time for the sunrise, doing a bit of early morning yoga, getting a hearty breakfast on the table, and checking for bombs under your car. It's a great way to add to the sense of well-being you're already feeling due to the 9 Essential Vitamins and Minerals infused into each, individual flake, puff, or crisp of your breakfast cereal by giant, energy-intensive industrial machines, and your first Valium of the day.

What else can you do to contribute to your sense of safety and security at the crack of dawn? How about taking that metal detector for a quick bomb-checking survey around the perimeter of your house? You can do that while the griddle's heating up. Or you might want to go online to the Department of Homeland Security's Terror Alert Page (www.dhs.gov/dhspublic/display?theme=29) to take a peek at the Current Threat Level. Or double-check the family arsenal to make sure all your weapons are where they should be, loaded and ready for action. Do it while the bacon's frying!

After breakfast you should make sure your Terrorist-Safe Reminder Tip List is securely fastened to your refrigerator and has not been tampered with.

Terrorist-Safe Reminder Tip List

— De-alphabetize your home library

— Remove doors from closets

— Change your Hotmail account password, then change it back

— Separate small pets from large ones

— Place jars of jam or jellies at rotating intervals of 8 to 10 meters throughout the house

— Never take the first taxicab in line

— Call random numbers from time to time

— Wear bright-colored clothing

— Stop using scented deodorants and soaps (specifically Avalanche or Cool Wave)

— Keep all lamps and lighting fixtures elevated

— Moisten walls

Hey kids: one of the items on this checklist is a bad idea. Can you tell which one?

Q: Are there any longer, general tips I should think about as I go about my day?

A: We're glad you asked. Here's a list of longer, general tips you should think about as you go about your day.

Longer, General Tips You Should Think about as You Go About Your Day

— Remember there's safety in numbers. Especially small ones, like five or seven.

— An ounce of prevention is worth a pound of cure and seven yards of regret and feeling sorry for yourself after your home and family have been destroyed.

— Dark deserted streets are places to avoid. Also, crowded streets with lots of people. Basically, avoid streets.

— Make sure you understand the underlying rationale for each security measure you take. Remember to ask yourself from time to time, "Why am I doing this?"

— Don't believe officials when they say, "Don't panic, everything's all right." Everything is not all right. They wouldn't be saying that if everything was all right.

— If your parking space at work says, "President," it might as well say, "Blow me up, please." Have it changed to "Average Loser Employee, Nobody Special Parks Here."

— Being too cautious never killed anyone, except my cousin Steve, who was too cautious to jump out of the plane on that skydiving trip, and then the plane crashed. And my other cousin, Marie, who was electrocuted by her high-tech home security system.

Q: What about suspicious behaviors to look out for?

Suspicious Behaviors to Look Out For

— A bunch of people enter a room and sit separately.

— A bunch of people get out of a cab and suddenly seem not to know each other.

— Out of the ordinary digging or trenching. (Terrorists love to dig and trench.)

— Somebody is photographing an ugly bridge. Why?

Since the beginning of the 21st century, computers and the Internet have become a source of information, entertainment, and a way to fulfill our emotional needs, which used to be met by interacting with one another. As they have become a part of your daily day, you must consider the subject of:

Cyber Security

You want to come up with a password that is not easy to hack (i.e., not common). For example, "Big Wiener" is the most commonly used password on the Internet. Over 3% of Americans use "Big Wiener" as their password. It's an obvious option for hackers. Many of you are running to your computers right now to change your password. But before you change it from "Big Wiener" to something else, here are some examples of good and bad passwords.

Your name is an example of a bad password. On the other hand, 76qR43iT is a good password. But don't use it, because we've just printed it in this book. Instead, use 84uM38oB.

When it becomes time to replace your computer—because the brand-new one you bought a month and a half ago is now so outdated that it no longer runs any current software, and when you bring it in for repairs the computer guys smile at each other and talk to you like you're an idiot—you must dispose of it properly to protect the private information stored on it.

Bad Way   **Good Way**

And now we will discuss how to tell if your drink has been poisoned.

Q: What does that have to do with this chapter?

A: What was this chapter supposed to be about?

Q: It was kind of vague.

A: Exactly.

How to Tell If Your Drink Has Been Poisoned

Give it to a friend you don't really like to try it first. (Wait about 75 seconds and observe any re-coloration of the facial area.)

If none of the suggestions in this chapter work for you or if you've already implemented them, how about another Valium?

Q: Which one of those terrorist-prevention tips was a bad idea?

A: Remove all doors from closets. That doesn't make any sense. Why would you do that?

Kidz Korner

Exit Strategy: The Maze

Help General Jibby lead the American Army out of Iraq!

Jibby   Koko

Chapter 20

Learning to Live after All Civilization Has Been Destroyed

The Family Disaster Kit: Essential Foods, Battery-Powered Video Games, Radiation-Resistant Hair Products

Well now, aren't you going to feel silly the morning after your development takes a direct nuclear hit from the ITAF (International Terrorist Air Force) and you haven't taken the time to prepare a disaster kit? You'll be raking through the rubble, looking for a bottle of drinking water or at least a fifth of Scotch, and you'll find nothing but shards of glass and the occasional remnant of the family cat. Don't look to your neighbors for help: the Funchellis will be staring at you through the gunsights of their AK-47s from behind their own, very well-fortified, very well-stocked bunker, and they're not about to share any of it with you.

Luckily, there's still time, exactly how much we can't say, but some. So get out your list and start thinking about what survival supplies are most essential to you and your particular needs. The Valium, of course, and a decent supply of hard liquor too, because without the basics you're not going to be capable of doing much about the rest of the stuff on the list. Then, it almost goes without saying: your own arsenal of AK-47s and other light arms to deal with the Funchellis if it turns out their bunker is less well supplied than they thought and they come running to you for help. A GPS device should be handy, not so much because it would be of any practical use, but because they're really neat and fun to play with. And since it could be many days or even weeks before emergency supplies reach your neighborhood, a battery-operated DVD player with your favorite pornography.

You'll discover that once you start thinking in an organized way about your survival issues, you won't actually need somebody else's advice about how to meet your needs. Our mission here is really to empower you to help yourself. At the same time, if you want a concrete suggestion or two, we'd suggest *Debbie Does Dallas* (you can't go wrong with the classics) and maybe *Barely Legal: The Bunny Storm Story.*

Redecorating Your Backyard Bomb Shelter: Good-Bye Formica, Hello Feng Shui!

Americans are a restless bunch, and chances are you're not living in the same place you lived in 50 years ago, if you were even alive 50 years ago, which you probably weren't because you look so young! In fact, you've lost weight, haven't you? Anyway, you look fabulous, and that bomb shelter in your backyard was probably built by someone else, and that person had really bad taste. Not to worry, it was the '50s. Everyone had bad taste.

The good news: you don't have to hire an expensive feng shui expert to ensure the energy fields are balanced in your shelter remodel, because this section is going to be your Personal Interior Design Consultant! And we have all the latest hints from our gay friends. Not that we, ourselves are gay. But we know homosexuals, and they have told us everything there is to tell about interior design, and we didn't even have to have sex with them. Honest.

Tip: Control the language. Call your bomb shelter a "club house" to make the kids more comfortable. "Everyone into the club house!" sounds so much better than "Everyone into the bomb shelter!" The only difference is that in this particular club house nobody gets to leave until all the radioactivity has passed.

A question which requires pre-catastrophe planning is: what kind of prints and artwork do I want inside my bomb shelter? A quick answer is still lifes (fruits, flowers), young ballerinas, landscapes. On the other hand, art you don't want includes screaming persons, saints being martyred, and anything that is just too weird. Here's a list:

YES	NO	MAYBE
Monet	Edvard Munch	Picasso (YES: *Dove of Peace*; NO: *Guernica*)
Manet	Goya	
Degas	Salvador Dali	
Van Gogh		
Renoir		

Another Tip from Our Gay Friends: If you're going to be spending the rest of your life in a small room with five other people, you'll want light-colored wallpaper.

Objection from Our Gay Friends: We're not actually gay, we just know a lot about interior design. We don't appreciate the stereotype.

Authors' Response to Gay Friends: Understood. We won't identify you as gay in the book then.

Key Items to Bring Along into the Bomb Shelter

Pet food—Even if you don't have a pet, just in case you run out of real food. Sure, it doesn't sound appetizing now, but when it's been two days since your last can of SpaghettiOs, you'll be glad it's there.

Can opener—If you forget it, you could draw straws to decide who has to go back into your radiation-infested home to get it, but then you'd have to remember to bring straws. You could open the can with a rock, but then you'd get SpaghettiOs all over the floor.

Photograph of Grandma—You're not going to be able to bring her with you into the bomb shelter (various reasons), so you'll want something to remember her by.

How to Defend Your Stash of Food and Water from Your Scavenger Neighbors, Now Deformed, Radiation-Mutilated Zombies

One of the most important things every serious counterterrorist should know is how to defend himself against radiation-mutilated neighbors. First, you must know a few things about radiation-mutilated neighbors:

1) They are likely to be ravenous and extremely hungry.
2) They will likely have forgotten all they once knew about morals and inhibitions.
3) They will eat your cat.

Knowing this about your new enemies, you are better prepared to anticipate their actions. You're also going to want to learn how to make a fire, to hunt, to decide which berries are OK to eat, to build a hut, and, eventually, to re-create a Nintendo Wii from common forest and post-nuclear disaster wreckage items. For more information on assembling a Nintendo Wii from scratch please see: www.assembleanintendoweiifromcom mon-forestandpostnucleardisastewreckageitems.com/coconut? howto+piecesofplastic?mud

Concentric Circles

Here's an important exercise for you and your family. In an emergency you must know in advance who gets priority spots in the bomb shelter.

Think of your responsibilities and familial priorities in terms of concentric circles revolving around you in the center. Locate various people in outwardly expanding concentric circles. Depending on the size of your bomb shelter and the amount of time you'll be able to leave the door open before it must be sealed, you may be able to incorporate two or three of the Priority Spheres.

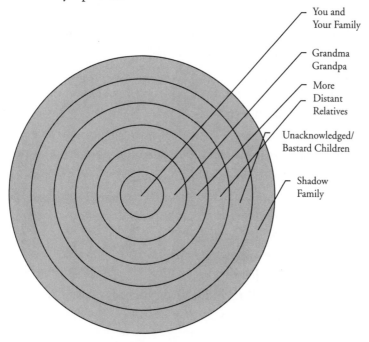

You and
Your Family

Grandma
Grandpa

More
Distant
Relatives

Unacknowledged/
Bastard Children

Shadow
Family

You are now ready for your first Terrorist Preparedness Quiz. Put away all notes and close this book. No, wait, don't close the book!

SPECIAL ALERT!

Terrorist Preparedness Quiz

Here are a few of the questions you will have to answer (they are not optional).

1) In 25 words or less: Why are you taking this quiz when you could be preparing to fight terrorism?

2) Yes or No: Do you fully support all the actions taken by your government in the War on Terrorism?
    2A) Why not?
    2B) What makes you think you're such an expert on foreign
    policy all of a sudden?

3) Fill in the blank: Terrorists do the evil things they do because they _____ freedom.

4) On the other hand, I, personally, _____ freedom.

5) Multiple choice: One of America's flaws is that it is:
    A) Run by the Jews.
    B) Tolerant of all religions, even the evil ones.
    C) There are no flaws.

6) Which of the following interactions with your neighbor is a Suspicious Interaction?
    A) Your neighbor knocks on your door, asks, "Can I borrow a cup of sugar?"
    B) Your neighbor knocks on your door, asks, "Can I borrow a cup of sugar, and do you have any enriched uranium?"

C) Your neighbor knocks on your door, asks, "Can I borrow a cup of sharp, metallic objects or other shrapnel which I can use to make the improvised explosive device I'm working on in my garage more deadly?"

If you answered B) and C) are Suspicious Interactions, you're already on your way to becoming an effective counterterrorist fighting machine!

Q: After reading this book so far, it seems to me that while terrorism is clearly something to be concerned about, maybe you guys are letting your fears get the best of you. Aren't there lots of other things just as threatening, if not more so? Is there any chance you're letting your paranoia about terrorism cloud your judgment to the point where you're no longer thinking rationally? If we allow terrorists to terrorize us, haven't the terrorists won?

A: We don't accept questions from terrorists.

Chapter 21

Training Your Dog: Detecting Explosives, Interrogating Detainees

We here at *The Ultimate Counterterrorist Home Companion* always like to think of dogs as our best friends. Mainly because our other best friends turned out to be such disloyal scum that even the thought of their names makes us want to break fragile kitchenware and maybe kill small animals. But small animals that are not dogs. Because we love dogs. And your dog can be an important weapon in your own personal struggle against terrorism.

Q: But what if my dog's a big fluffy, rich-white-person dog who is not very ferocious and is sometimes frightened by even medium-sized cats?

A: Why would you buy a dog like that in times like these? Seriously, have you been living under a rock? Well, at least most terrorists are like people, afraid of dog bites, even from small, fluffy dogs.

Q: What if my dog's typical reaction to an intruder would be better described as more of a licking than a biting.

A: Studies have shown that licking is considerably less of a deterrent to terrorist intruders than biting. But at least a strong and ferocious bark may be comparatively effective.

Q: What if my dog's ferocious bark would be better described as a pathetic whimper?

A: Goddamnit!

Q: Did I do something wrong?

A: No, it's not you. It's just been a long day.

Q: I understand.

A: I'm sorry.

Q: I'm sorry, too.

Dogs are like your friends, not good at things like math, science, and remembering not to lick strangers, but they excel in other areas. In the case of your friends: throwing up on command. In the case of dogs: smelling.

Did you know that your dog can recognize the scent of anthrax? Training is not difficult. Remember that dogs respond to positive reinforcement, so keep dog biscuits around for rewards, just like you do with Grandpa. (Don't let your neighbors know you're using dog biscuits with Grandpa.)

Anthrax Training for Your Dog

Sugar   Flour   Anthrax

After training, be sure to dispose of your anthrax using safe techniques and procedures.

Tip: Be sure to remember which is which so you don't end up with Double Chocolate Anthrax Cake and lose a perfectly good pound of sugar or flour.

In the world of counterterrorism, you never know who to trust. Even your closest friends could and in all likelihood will betray you. That is another reason your dog is your number one ally in this battle. No matter how bad things get, you know your dog will never sell your home security information to the Afghanis for drug money. You know that your dog will never have a change of heart, and suddenly realize that the true path to salvation is to establish an Islamic amirate, which adheres rigorously to the ordinances of sharia law. Dogs just don't think like that.

But people do think like that. And even your loved ones can change. Or maybe you think you're talking to a loved one, but it's really a terrorist in a mask, like in *Mission Impossible*. That's why you must never divulge any truly sensitive material to anyone other than your dog.

But what if you do begin to question your dog's loyalty, or worse, question if your dog may himself be a terrorist? That is when we would recommend that you put down this book and seek professional help because you have officially taken this whole counterterrorism thing too far. It's one thing to train your dog to sniff out terrorists, detonate land mines, gather information, and conduct antiterrorist night rounds, but it's another thing entirely to question his patriotism. And this book will not tolerate that kind of blasphemy. In fact, you should go apologize to your dog right now for even reading this paragraph.

Now, how about a poem?

Counterterrorist Pet-Related Poem

Oh, the innocence of the dog,

Who knows not the stakes,

Who knows only the doggie treat at the end of the desired behavior.

Catch a frisbee, sniff the mail, bite the crotch area of a detainee,

It's all a game.

Oh, the innocence of the dog.

Q: Why is there a poem in this chapter?

A: What, you didn't like it?

Q: It's not that I didn't like it. It just seemed a little out of place.

A: That's your opinion.

Q: Are you still mad about before?

A: No, not at all.

Q: You are still mad!

Conclusion

In sum, it's worth noting we can actually learn a lot about terrorists by studying our dogs, because terrorists and dogs have a lot in common. They tend to be hairy, speak English poorly, and can lick their own balls. So spend more time with your dog.

Q: Why does this chapter have a conclusion, when none of the others do?

A: We're sorry, this chapter has already concluded.

Chapter 22

Making Your Own Color-Coded Terrorism Alert Chart: Is Heightened Danger of Radiation Exposure More of a Lavender or a Robin's Egg Blue?

You, of course, do not have the kind of resources available to your government, specifically your Department of Homeland Security, which now has so many resources to draw on that it's becoming a major supplier of waste, fraud, and mismanagement to the nation after only a few years in existence! So naturally, the DHS has this fancy fear chart with a lot of neat colors, while you have this crappy little cardboard thing with a movable arrow, which keeps falling off the goddamn chart. That's really pathetic. You ought to be ashamed of yourself.

Yeah, yeah. You don't have the budget. But you managed to find enough money to go out to dinner at Chez Very Expensive the other night, didn't you? And somehow you paid for those useless "decorative pillows" that you can't even use like a normal pillow but are just there to look at, like someone's going to be looking in your bedroom, admiring the pillows.

Do you think Paul Revere "couldn't find" the money for his Wake-Up-You-Numbskulls-The-British-Are-Coming Advance Warning System? Do you think FEMA "couldn't find" the money for their highly effective Pre-Katrina Advance Warning System? Do you believe the Kareem-Magic Lakers of 1988 could take the Kobe-Shaq Lakers of 2002?

So basically, your own personal Fear Chart will not be as ultimate as ours. Don't feel bad, we are experts. We're sure that during the time we were working hard to become experts, the time you spent getting drunk and stoned was enjoyable.

Here is a sample Home Fear Alert Chart you can use as the basis for your own, personalized Fear Chart. Or you could just steal it.

We strongly recommend that you use shades of grey instead of actual colors, because your publisher will probably not want to invest the amount of money necessary to make an actual color-coded chart at this point. This doesn't mean your color selection needs to be less creative. You still need to select the shades of grey that best represent the level of fear appropriate for the given circumstances. In our chart

HOME FEAR
ALERT CHART

STARTLED

JUMPY

SKITTISH

JITTERY

SCARED

ALARMED

COMPLETELY
FLUSTERED AND PUT
OUT IN EVERY WAY

we have chosen Eggshell White, Cement Grey, Misty Afternoon Grey, Pebblestone Creek Grey, Light Black, Dark Black, and Midnight Black.

Determining the appropriate fear level for a given day should be based on a careful assessment of the volume of chatter in your neighborhood. Go out on your porch and do some surveillance: are people stopping to chat with each other on the street, or are they ignoring each other and avoiding eye contact as you would normally expect. Do your family members appear to be acknowledging each other's presence? Time to ratchet up the Fear Alert Level.

Q: Could you define "chatter"?

A: To utter a succession of quick, inarticulate speech-like sounds, as monkeys, terrorists, and certain birds.

SPECIAL ALERT!

Antiterrorist Fitness

People often ask, "What kind of shape do I have to be in to be an effective counterterrorist?" The answer is nothing out of the ordinary—a sensible program of diet, exercise, and sporadic bulimia should do the trick.

Take a look at these actual photographs of two classic American sexual icons, Kate Moss and Karl Rove.[1]

Which would you guess is better fit for the War on Terrorism?

Karl Rove   **Kate Moss**

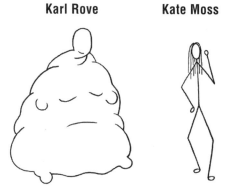

We in the counterterrorist industry would consider Karl Rove **not fit for terrorism fighting**, whereas Kate Moss is **ready for action**.

Kate Moss's fitness allows her several opportunities to be an effective counterterrorist which Karl Rove doesn't have. For example, if she is taken captive she has a substantially higher chance of slipping through the bars. She can also use air currents to **float away**. On the other hand, Karl can neither slip through the bars nor use air currents in his escape.

---

[1] photo by Bryan Duddles

In the event of a terrorist intrusion, Kate Moss has the ability to conceal her person by **blending into the wall**, whereas Karl Rove would be unable to blend in with anything other than a giant glob of cookie dough.

Make sure your children know that you approve of the way Kate Moss looks, and that you expect them to do what it takes to look like her.

That was Section Three. Coming up next—you won't want to miss: Section Four. You won't believe what happens in Chapter 25. Plus, our exclusive interview with Chapter 23. That's all coming up and more in Section Four, so stay with us.

All the Other Chapters That Didn't Appear in Section One, Two, or Three

SPECIAL ALERT!

Halftime Mid-Book Pep Talk

Some of you read the first half of this book like you didn't care if the terrorists won. Some of you read it like it was somebody *else's* job to beat the terrorists.

Anybody think that? How about you, O'Sullivan—is that what you think? Hernandez? Washington? Anybody want to step forward and say what *other* reader is going to win this one for us?

Think about Darren, the intern who got hit by a FedEx truck while going out to get us coffee and sprinkled doughnuts at Krispy Kreme and who's now in a coma. He's in a coma so we could get this book to you.

OK then. When we go out there into the second half of this book, we want to see each and every one of you giving 110% on *every* page!

So forget about the damn score and read with some pride!

Q: You know, technically speaking, it's really more like the end of the third quarter than halftime, and usually there isn't a big speech like that at the end of the third quarter, just so you know.

A: If you're gonna call yourself "Q," which presumably stands for "question," you're really going to have to stop making statements, or we are going to have to start calling you "S," and that would just be confusing for everyone who didn't specifically read this halftime pep talk.

Q: Third quarter pep talk.

A: Yes Q, third quarter pep talk. Thank you, Q.

Chapter 23

Surveillance Cameras: Deterring Nuclear Attacks and Finding Out Who's Been Stealing Your Newspaper

The War on Terrorism is about information. Secrets and secrecy can no longer be tolerated if we are to put an end to this dangerous new fad. You need to know what's going on beyond the boundaries of where your God-given eyes can see. What exactly goes on in your neighbor's house behind closed doors? What do the Goldsteins really do during their "Chanukah" celebrations? What kind of chemical agents go into the process of making unleavened bread? What is that little thing they spin around? How hot does your neighbor's wife like the water to be when she is showering? What really is the password to your neighbor's wireless Internet connection (which you can see would work perfect for you every day if you could only figure out that damn password)?

To answer these questions, you will need to construct a highly intricate network of surveillance cameras in your neighborhood. Some people will always complain that when you or your government starts doing little things like putting up surveillance cameras everywhere, it is an "invasion of privacy." But really, privacy is only something people care about when they have something to hide. So the next time someone complains that this or that is an invasion of privacy, what you should really ask them in return is, "What is it you don't want me to know?" Then set up a system of surveillance cameras and wiretapping equipment and start tearing apart their home to find out.

What constitutes actionable intelligence? Here are some things to look out for:

Mobile Weapons Volvo

Chemical Weapons Stockpile

Nuclear Device Construction Manual

If your surveillance leads you to determine that you must physically enter your neighbor's home to gather more evidence, you should not go in without an exit strategy.

Exit Strategies to Consider

— Bring other neighbors into the house to stabilize the situation.

— Redeploy to the front lawn creating an "over-the-horizon" quick reaction force in case you have to go back in.

— Stand down as your neighbors stand up.

— Leave it up to some future neighborhood leader.

But suppose the elusive and deceptive practices of your neighbor make it difficult to get your inspection team in on the ground. Keeping a watchful eye on your own family is one thing, but knowing what's going on behind your neighbor's thick hedge and closed doors is another. It's simple enough to install a tiny surveillance camera in your son's bedroom while he's safely occupied in high school or doing drugs in the alley behind the mall, but how to access the Funchellis' den?

One method is sex, so often the gateway to information. Like so many married men, Roberto Funchelli spends many idle hours fantasizing about hot, extramarital affairs, and probably at least some of those fantasies have focused on you. Next time your husband is off on a business trip, arrange to intercept Roberto on his way home. Explain that your husband is out of town, and that you're such a ninny about plumbing you just don't know what to do about your balky toilet, and when the back door closes, don't waste time.

Once you've reduced Roberto to a trembling puddle of lust, exploit your advantage to gain intelligence about him and his family, teasing and toying with his desires, his guilt, and his fear of exposure.

Just remember that you're doing all of this to defend your country. So if, while performing your patriotic duty, it amuses you to make Roberto bark like a dog, go ahead, you deserve it.

Q: Is this all a metaphor for how Hans Blix used his sexual appeal to gain unprecedented access for the United Nations weapons inspectors?

A: Yes.

Kidz Korner

Help Rescue Jennifer from the Terrorists Maze

Jibby   Koko

Fourteen-year-old Jennifer, whose parents carelessly allowed her to go to the mall with her friends, has been captured by terrorists and is being held prisoner in the basement of a French restaurant.

Help Jibby and Koko rescue Jen, before she's drugged and bundled off on the next flight to Peshawar, where she'll be claimed as a bride by a top Al Qaeda leader!

Chapter 24

Intelligence Gathering: Suspicious Organizations, Informant Networks— Is Water-Boarding One Word or Two?

As we've discovered as a result of our adventure in Iraq (what a great learning experience!), there's nothing more important than intelligence. Not in the smarty-pants, high-SAT-score sense that real Americans hate, but in the real, everyday sense of intelligence, the kind of truthfulness/honesty you only get from somebody whose fingers you've just broken one by one.

So: how do we gather intelligence in our own communities? The answer is, the same way our government gathers intelligence in our nation and around the world: recruiting reliable informants, listening in on conversations, torturing suspicious persons, deciding what we want to know, trying to find as much evidence as we can to support the conclusions we've already made, and sometimes just wishing or praying hard enough that something we would like to be true actually is true.

While we may lack the massive resources of our government, we can certainly take advantage of some of the simpler interrogation methods we've learned so much about in recent years. Water-boarding for example, can be mastered in just hours. And if torture is against the moral standards of your particular household, you can always render the suspect to the household of your uncle "Crazy Charlie" for more effective intelligence gathering. This chapter provides instructions for the beginner on similar tricks of the trade, as well as helping you to develop your own spy network and infiltrate such organizations as the ACLU, peace committees, and gay and lesbian groups. (Don't worry: we'll show you how to be among homosexuals without becoming one!)

Q: Let me stop you right there and ask you to expand on that last thought before you get so wrapped up in talking about all the things you're going to say in the chapter, that you don't actually provide any information about anything. How do I spend time among homosexuals without becoming one?

A: Don't make eye contact. Try to establish a perimeter around yourself of at least two to three feet. Don't exchange names, phone numbers, or e-mail addresses. If you feel yourself becoming gay, leave the room immediately.

Q: Another quick question: what does this gay stuff have to do with anything?

A: Hey, you brought it up, not us. We were trying to talk about intelligence gathering.

Q: Isn't that sort of like the previous chapter?

A: Well, what do *you* want to talk about?

Q: I'd like to talk about spam e-mail. Don't you hate that?

A: Yes, and thanks for bringing it up. Getting back to intelligence gathering:

Say you hear there's an ACLU meeting in your neighborhood. You decide to attend to see what the freedom-haters are up to. But you have to blend in, know the lingo. Here are some tips:

— Use the word "Comrade" to refer to other members.

— When the conversation turns to the violent overthrow of our government, don't let on that it disturbs you.

— Be aware of the dates and pronunciation of all major Jewish holidays.

— Also all the significant dates in the history of France.

But how to blend in at a Greenpeace meeting?

— Bring a bathing suit.

— Accept whatever drugs they offer and try to keep your cool. Don't worry, most of these drugs wear off after a while.

— Know your way around a bongo drum.

At the Peace Rally:

— Know the second half of the most common chants. When the leader goes, "Fee, fi, fo, fitler," you go "George Bush is worse than Hitler!" Try to sound angry.

You should also be comfortable chanting in other languages. You may be expected to yell:

— *"¡Si, se puede!"* which is German for "Down with America!"

When somebody asks, "Why are you taking my picture?" You say, "Because, man, this is so beautiful, man, people coming together, man."

When you go home and "come down" from all those drugs they gave you, write all the names down, and match them with the photographs you've taken.

Chapter 25

Baking Your Way to Homeland Security: Pineapple Upside-Down Flag Cake and Other Patriotic Arts & Crafts

We can't all be quarterbacks and wide receivers; some of us have bad ankles, others of us are just so uncoordinated that when we touch a football, even if we're just trying to move it from the middle of the living room floor to a safe closet, someone from the other team is likely to take it from us and score a game-winning touchdown. But that's the great thing about football. There are also important positions on the team for people with artistic talent, namely, the cheerleaders. Cheerleaders capture the spirit of the team, bring motivation to the players, and remind us of how to spell tricky words like, D-E-F-E-N-S-E and G-O-W-I-L-D-C-A-T-S, which we realize a few minutes later was really two words which is why we were so confused.

The point is, not all of us have to be the fighters on the ground to help our neighborhood fight terrorism. In this chapter we discuss all the ways that you can spread the patriotic spirit from your home to your block to your whole city. Everything from recipes and interior design ideas to patriotic hats and beach towels to expressive patriotic painting, sculpting, and shower singing.

Q: But what patriotic songs should I sing in the shower? I only have a limited amount of time before the hot water runs out, especially if somebody else in my family has hogged up all the hot water before I even get to start mine.

A: It depends on the range of your voice. However, here is a list ranking the most patriotic songs in order of patriotism:

The Most Patriotic Songs Graph

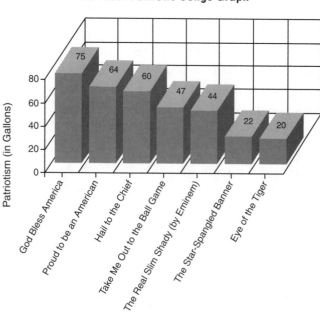

And don't underestimate the value of patriotic artistry. Many people say that had John Ashcroft focused on his patriotic singing career instead of involving himself in the more tangible aspects of governance, the office of the Attorney General of the United States would hold more dignity, and the world as a whole would be a better place today.

Q: But aren't those people terrorists?

A: Yes, and we're glad you brought that up, because that's what this chapter is about: terrorism, and combating it expressively.

And remember, you don't even have to make something that is overtly patriotic in nature. As long as you create your piece of art while thinking about your own personal patriotism, the artwork will reflect your dedication to your country, and will lift the spirits of the entire community. It's like the ripple effect or the domino theory, or a very infectious epidemic, like smallpox or the black plague.

Anyway, every little thing helps!

Special alert: it's been a long time since 9/11 and people are beginning to take down the flags on their front lawn and cars. If enough people take down their flags, we could be vulnerable to another attack. You don't have to wait for another attack to become patriotic. You can be preemptively patriotic, not reactively patriotic. Flag 'em here so we don't have to "flag" 'em over there. The same applies to flag cakes. So go to your kitchen RIGHT NOW, and bake a flag!

Q: But I don't have a recipe.

A: Recipe For Pineapple Upside-Down Flag Cake:
— Melt a stick of butter in a pan, and add a cup of brown sugar, trying not to burn everything.

— Open a can of pineapple slices, dump them into a flag-shaped baking pan, and also put a bunch of maraschino cherries in there.

— Have a drink, you deserve one.

— Take six eggs, separated, a cup of flour, a cup of sugar— oh, hell, just get a goddamn cake mix.

— Have another drink. You've saved yourself a lot of time and trouble, especially if you got the kind of cake mix where you don't even have to add an egg, just water. Nobody's going to know, OK?

— Just add the water to the mix, or whatever it tells you to do on the box, and pour the cake mix over the pineapple gook.

— You forgot to preheat the oven to 325 degrees. So do that, and have another drink while you're waiting.

— Put the pan into the oven, set the timer. Drink at will.

— Was that the timer, or is somebody at the door? Well, you better just take the cake out of the oven, flip it upside down onto a plate. If it was somebody at the door, they will eventually go away.

— Put a bunch of red, white, and blue frosting on it, and some little flags.

Q: But what if I don't have the right colored frosting to make a flag cake?

A: You go to bake with the colored frosting you have, not the colored frosting you want.

Chapter 26

What Are You Good At? What You Can Do to Combat Terrorism as a Lawyer, Actor, or Someone Who Just Knows Their Way Around a Kiln

We can all use the skills we've developed in our professions to help fight the War on Terror. For example, we as authors had previously only written silly, useless, non-terrorism-fighting comedy books. But when we heard our nation calling, we began to use the skills we've developed to help fight the great battle of our time against our most threatening enemy in history—big losers who hang around chat rooms.

In this chapter we look at some of the ways that you can help fight the War on Terror using whatever skills you've developed in your professional and personal life. For example, if you're in the media, you can make sure to remind people constantly of the War on Terrorism by overhyping even the least credible terror alerts and investigations. This way, even when it turns out that you spent two days nonstop covering a potential terrorist organization that turned out to be a yoga club with several members who have beards and may or may not have relatives who live in Venezuela, you helped remind your country that it is still under attack and never to forget to live in fear, *and* you boosted your ratings big time!

If you're in publishing, you can help by publishing books by Ann Coulter, a lively yet responsible voice from slightly right-of-center on the political spectrum, to balance out the well-known liberal bias of the media.

What If You're Just a Soccer Mom?

No prob. There's lots of skills you've picked up at the soccer games that can help. (Most of these correlations are obvious; you've probably already noticed the stark similarities between fighting terrorism and the AYSO.)

Skills You Already Have	Related Skills That Can Help in the Long War
Translating what your daughter's Lithuanian coach is saying.	Translating terrorist videos.
Bringing a lawn chair.	Anticipating insurgent tactics.
Learning the names of all the kids on the team.	Familiarizing yourself with at least two of the major religious/ethnic groups in countries you're invading.
Pretending to know the rules.	Organizing an extraordinary rendition.
Pretending to care.	Putting a flag outside your house.

Skills You Already Have	Related Skills That Can Help in the Long War
Naming a group of six-year-olds "The Annihilators."	Calling the destruction of your core values the Patriot Act.
Driving around with five screaming kids.	Building up torture tolerance.
Getting your kid on the All Star Team.	Getting some of that government antiterrorist money for your neighborhood.
Spending your entire Saturday every weekend in the burning sun as little children chase a ball up and down the field never getting anywhere amidst lots of screaming and sprained ankles.	The war in Iraq.

But what if you're not a soccer mom? There are also other professions, and ways to use your professional skills to combat terrorism. Here is a list of all of them:

Profession	What You Can Do
Artist/musician	Quit now while you're still young and get a real job.
Teacher	(See above)
Journalist	Don't write articles which embolden the enemy, undermine the troops, or embolden the underminers.

TV executive	Put more shows like *24* on the air, which remind us that we are under attack by terrorists all the time, and the only person on earth who is not a terrorist is Keifer Sutherland, and maybe he is, too.
Telemarketer	Please stop calling me.

Q: My career was not mentioned in your list of all careers. Does that mean it's not a legitimate career?

A: You said it, not us.

Q: But didn't you imply it by not mentioning my career?

Everyone can use their skills to help. Everyone from the gardener, to the mailman, to your friend Steve, who's best known for his ability to belch the alphabet while crushing beer cans against his uniquely large and protruding left hip bone.

It just takes a little know-how. And Steve, if you're reading this, please contact us ASAP and let us know how the heck you do that thing with the belching. Does it have something to do with diaphragm control? Because then opera stars could do it, since they have very excellent diaphragm control, and they could, like, belch the entire *La Traviata,* and how cool would *that* be?

Chapter 27

Varying Your Routine— Different Routes to School, Church on Thursday, Starting with Dessert

If there's anything your typical terrorist thrives on, it's predictability. Today you can pretty much assume you're being watched, and not just by your government. Your government is listening in on your phone calls, reading your mail, studying your financial transactions and generally spying on you in a good way—to make sure that you're not a terrorist. But the terrorists are spying on you in a bad way—to spot your vulnerability to attack. To whatever extent your daily routine is the same from one day to the next, you are a sitting duck. Quack, quack!

Get out of bed at the same time every morning? Quack! Park your car in the same place at night? Quack! Put your dishes away in the same place all the time? Quack! Have sex in the "missionary" position repeatedly, with about the same amount of time spent on foreplay? Quack, quack, quack!

Clearly, you need to alter your routines, especially your sexual routine. If you're that predictable, *nobody* is getting off, and that includes you, your spouse, the government, and the terrorists. So, for mercy sakes, change it up now and then, try "the forklift" once in a while, or "the flying bookmark."

Changing your routine is easier than you think. For example, we've been writing in English up to now, which is predictable. However, aber abseits wer ist's? Im Gebüsch verliert sich der Pfad. Hinter ihm schlagen Die Sträuche zusammen, Das Gras steht wieder auf, Die Öde verschlingt ihn. Ach, wer heilet die Schmerzen Des, dem Balsam zu Gift ward? Der sich Menschenhaß Aus der Fülle der Liebe trank? Erst verachtet, nun ein Verächter, Zehrt er heimlich auf Seinen eigenen Wert In ungenugender Selbstsucht. Ist auf deinem Psalter, Vater der Liebe, ein Ton Seinem Ohre vernehmlich, So erquicke sein Herz! Öffne den umwölkten Blick Über die tausend Quellen Neben dem Durstenden.

In der Wüste!

Using this method you make the terrorist's job more difficult, and your life more exciting. Just when the terrorists think they've begun to understand your behavior, you suddenly ma che vi fece, o stelle, la povera dircea, che tante unite sventure contro lei! Voi, che inspirate i casti affetti alle nostr'alme; voi, che al pudico imeneo, foste presenti, difendetelo, o numi: io mi confondo. M'oppresse il colpo a segno, che il cor mancommi, e si smarrì l'ingegno. Sperai vicino il lido, crudei calmato il vento, ma trasportar mi sento fra le tempeste ancor. E da uno scoglio infido mentre salvar mi voglio, urto in un altro scoglio del primo assai peggior.

Sometimes it's good to return to your routine momentarily, but you should consider doing whatever it was you were doing normally with some kind of new angle. Start with your left foot for a change, watch CNN instead of Fox, or, if that's too much to ask, watch Sean Hannity instead of Bill O'Reilly.

A: For example, wouldn't it be surprising to start with the answer instead of the question?

Q: *At this point, no, it's not surprising.*

A: You're just being grumpy because you don't speak Italian.

SPECIAL ALERT!

Personal Risk Assessment Assessment

In assessing your Personal Risk Assessment, you need to determine how you personally rank as a potential terrorist target. Ask yourself these questions, and add up your scores (start with zero, no offense):

What's your Societal Position?
— Are you Someone Special (+10) or are you Kind of a Loser (+7)?
— Do you hold high-ranking office (+15) or do you sometimes misspell "office" (+9)?

What risky behaviors might be putting you at risk?
— Do you get your water from a municipal water service? Yes (+15), No (+9), or Not Sure (+23)
— Do you work outside your home? Yes (+20) or No (+15)
— Do you eat food that at one point may have been handled by another person? Yes (+11) or No (+6)

Are you a target for abduction?
— Has anyone ever asked you, "What's your sign?" or "Do you come here often?"

Q: Wasn't that person flirting with me?

A: Do you look like Angelina Jolie or Brad Pitt?

Q: No.

A: Then, no (+16).

Add up your number, multiply by three and assess your Risk Assessment. If your number is high (like 172), you should consider changing your behavioral activities, or retaking the test and lying.

Several Chapters That Would Have Been More Appropriate for Section Three Although We Overlooked It at the Time

Chapter 28

The False Alarm Chapter: Fireworks, Jackhammers, and Misplaced Keys

It might not seem like it, here on the ground in the middle of the war, but there is a chance that we can be *too* paranoid. While it is clear that the threat of terrorism has affected our institutions in diverse ways, we can't blame terrorism for everything that goes wrong in our lives. Surely we can prove that there is a causal relationship between our struggle with terrorism and a sagging economy, global warming, and Hollywood's obnoxious obsession with turning old movies into new movies that aren't as good as the old ones which weren't really all that great to begin with.

But can we then go as far as to blame terrorists for our children's fascination with violent television, or loud noises we hear in the middle of the night that sound exactly like antiaircraft missiles, but in fact turn out to be thunder? Should we work ourselves into a state of panic every time we hear firecrackers, see Arab people, misplace our keys, or notice a crooked painting in our living room that really was straight 15 minutes ago when we went into the kitchen?

The answer is, maybe, but probably not. In this lighter, more upbeat, chapter we will discuss and illustrate the many things, including baldness, the unbelievable number of years since the Chicago Cubs have won a World Series, cellulite, car alarms, and certain members of your family, for whom terrorism is probably not to blame. (But maybe is.)

As recently as a few months ago, alert citizens in Boston, Massachusetts, discovered several suspicious devices with blinking lights on them. They immediately called authorities, who acted quickly. In a well-coordinated response, officials shut down the major arteries of that city as well as tunnels and bridges. Bombs squads were sent, and one of the devices was blown up.

As it turned out, the devices were advertisements for a TV cartoon show on The Cartoon Network called *Aqua Teen Hunger Force*. But that's not the point. Had they indeed been nuclear devices, the citizens of Boston would have been protected. Meanwhile, when similar devices were deployed in New York City, the only response from citizens there was to steal them as souvenirs. Had they been bombs, New York might have been utterly destroyed.

Q: How can I tell the difference between an advertisement for a TV cartoon show and a nuclear bomb?

A: Study the following illustrations carefully:

Not a Bomb   **Bomb**

Also, our terrorist movie research has shown that bombs almost invariably have colored wires on them, one of which, being cut, will defuse the bomb, the other being cut, will detonate the bomb. Hint: go with your gut. Our research shows that it works 95% of the time. If, on the other hand, just as you're about to snip the wire, there's a sudden cut to a much longer, wider shot, that would be an indication you're cutting the wrong wire. This typically happens at the beginning of the movie. Try not to cut any bomb wires in the first 15 minutes of a movie. If you can make it through the first action sequence, your chance of picking the right wire goes up exponentially.

But we must always treat false alarms as real alarms no matter what type of cartoon they end up being. Why? Well, have you heard the lesser-known, longer version of Aesop's story, "The Boy Who Cried Wolf," which was incidentally originally titled, "The Boy Who Cried Wolf and the Silly Villagers Who Ignored Him and Were Later Devoured by the Wolf and All His Wolf Friends Once They Realized That the Village Was No Longer on Alert"?

It is arguable that original title was not as catchy and portable as the modern version, but it is worth noting. We can think of the wolves in this case as the terrorists, the villagers as all Americans, and the shepherd boy as Cable News.

(Note: Aesop's editors found the original version too violent and not suitable for a children's story. Aesop maintains to this day the story would have been more successful as he intended it.)

Anyway, this is why even today, we as Americans have to take all alarms seriously: so that we are not eaten by wolves.

Kidz Korner

Color This Important Part of Our Counterterrorist History (stay within the lines)

Jibby   Koko

Chapter 29

Days to Be Extra Scared: Holidays, Millennia, Days of Indictments of Major Congressional Leaders

We all know that there are certain days of the year when terrorists are more likely to strike than others. Whatever their reasons, be it jealousy of the Christmas spirit, anger over never getting invited to cool New Year's Eve parties, or bewilderment over the whole concept of the Easter Bunny, we should all be extra worried around times of celebration. What this worrying should look like in practical terms is up to you: an extra eggnog perhaps, crossing your fingers when the clock strikes 12 on New Year's Eve, or putting yourself in a Valium-induced hibernation during the month of December, whatever works.

In this chapter we will discuss specific strategies based on the unique threats associated with holidays, large gatherings of Boy Scouts, and last but not least, the day after the announcement of some piece of very bad news for the current in-power political party, whichever that may be. No one knows why these days are so likely to be days of raised terrorist concern; coincidence, something to do with the alignment of

Uranus, or a bizarre fascination amongst the terrorists with bailing out American political leaders from potentially weeks of bad news when they get caught doing something very bad.

Since we don't know, we have to assume that it has something to do with the alignment of Uranus, since that was the only option involving a word that could potentially mean "your asshole" if pronounced the right way. However, alternate explanations will also be considered in this chapter, and then dismissed. Sometimes we feel like nobody really reads our books. That they just buy the book for the cover or title, and never really open it. Or maybe flip around a little, then resell it on Amazon. Are you really reading this? Oh good. Some people (not you) just look at the pictures and never get around to reading the carefully constructed prose. But not you, sir or madam. You will be prepared for the next terrorist attack. Way more than those other people.

Q: But how does all this theoretical talk affect my actual New Year's Eve party?

A: Poppers are no longer advisable, they make your guests too jittery. Also, the sound of kazoos can be easily mistaken for all sorts of terrorist activities. When the ball begins to drop on TV and the countdown starts at 10, you should be braced in a survival position in a doorjamb or under a table. When you count down, it shouldn't be in a drunken, sloppy, celebratory manner, it should be more of a countdown-to-launch, self-destruct, holy-shit-we're-all-about-to-die-style cadence. (Note for Jewish people: the traditional mashed-potato fight should not begin until 20 minutes after midnight.)

Q: How does it affect my Easter party?

A: Less colored eggs, more assault weapons.

Q: What about Christmas?

A: You should not allow your fears to dampen the Christmas spirit. Just take a few common-sense precautions at this time of giving and wonder.

1) Don't assume footsteps on your roof are necessarily Santa and his reindeer.
2) Don't let anyone else handle your presents.
3) Don't leave presents unattended at any time.
4) Don't joke about "bombs" in your Christmas presents—family personnel are trained to react.

We asked a random sample of 750 terrorists what their favorite holidays were. Here are the top holidays and most commonly cited reasons why.

Favorite Holiday	Reasons Why
New Year's Eve	Guard down, decadent crusaders too drunk to care.
Chanukah	Especially hate the Jews.
Halloween	Easy to disguise self as goblin, Captain Jack Sparrow, or fairy princess, blend in, take advantage of general confusion.
Easter	Those chocolate eggs with the creamy stuff inside: can't get enough.
Passover	Jew-hating is not a once-a-year kind of thing.
Super Bowl Sunday	Still angry about wardrobe malfunction.
Valentine's Day	Tired of not having a Valentine.
St. Patrick's Day	Hate the Irish.

Day of the Dead   Love the title.

Groundhog Day   Thought Bill Murray was better
                             in *Ghostbusters*.

Of course, there's also Earth Day, Mother's Day, Father's Day, and Grandparent's Day, not to mention the other 350 days, which are at least as dangerous, if not more so because they're not the days you expect a terrorist attack. So there's a lot to think about.

Q: What, exactly, is terrorism?

A: *Terrorism* (official government definition): Anything that constitutes a threat and/or displeasurable influence on or in regards to any institution/policy deemed non-terrorist/valuable, or could be in any way disruptive to the general well-being of such institution, as to be describably problematic, so on and so forth.

Q: Wow. Now that I know what the definition of terrorism is, I realize that my group or organization may be under more of a terrorist threat than I had previously thought. Can I get some of the government counterterrorist funding?

A: Your government is happy to distribute funds to fight terrorism. What's your organization? A yoga meditation group? Is the yoga meditation group across the street—which has been siphoning off your members—possibly a terrorist organization? Is your Kangaroo Conservation Center not getting DHS funding because it's all going to the Kangaroo Conservation Center in Dawsonville, Georgia, which (and in no way is this a lie) recently received federal antiterrorist funding? Is your Little League team feeling financially intimidated in your fundraising efforts by the Girl Scouts and their cookie drive? Are the Girls Scouts possibly a terrorist organization? Check definition above. You will probably find the answer is yes.

Chapter 30

Is It Possible for America Itself to Engage in Terrorism?

No.

Chapter 31

Thinking Like a Terrorist: Freedom Hating, Grudge Holding, and the Whole 72 Virgins-in-Paradise Thing

Oh, boy. This is tough. Because you are definitely *not* a terrorist. And we, the authors of this book are definitely, *definitely* not terrorists. And just to be clear for any agents of the Department of Homeland Security or National Joint Terrorism Task Force, neither you the reader, nor we the authors, are terrorists.

That said, in order to defeat them (the terrorists) we have to learn how to think like them. A simple exercise is to pretend that you hate freedom. People who hate freedom pretty much hate everything and everyone. Let's see if we can get you hating everyone as quickly and easily as possible. Try this: think of someone you'd like to kill, like your boss or your father-in-law, and pretend that you felt that way about everyone. Recall some of the ways in the past you've imagined killing your boss. If you're like most people, you've probably imagined lowering your boss slowly into a pit full of hungry alligators. Or, if you're a little on the crazy side, bears.

You may never learn to hate freedom the way a terrorist does because you don't have the cerebral structure of a terrorist.

For example, you may not have the "hate freedom synapse," illustrated here:

Why They Hate Us

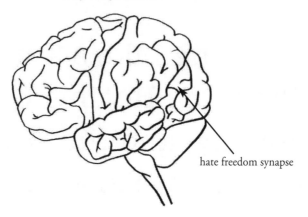

hate freedom synapse

Still, you'll want to do your best to learn what it's like to hate freedom. Try hate by association: put a picture of something you currently hate, like your boss, on an American flag, and practice associating the two ideas together to the point where you begin hating them both simultaneously. Or periodically play our national anthem and poke yourself in the eye whenever you hear it. You'll be surprised how quickly just the thought of that song will bring a sense of dread.

Another example is the virgins-in-paradise thing. Most Americans are not particularly into virgins, with the possible exception of some very devout Christian fundamentalists who have probably stopped reading this book by now, in the unlikely event they ever started. Americans believe (and this applies to all genders) that a certain amount of experience is desirable in a lover. Maybe not *that* much experience, but *some* experience. As our beloved Founding Father Benjamin Franklin put it in his justly famous essay, "On Choosing a Mistress": "the Pleasure, or Corporal Enjoyment with an old Woman is at least equal, and frequently superior, every Knack being by Practice capable of improvement." Not that we're suggesting sex with old people, but you catch the drift.

If the suicide bomber is himself also a virgin, a reasonable assumption, it's like two people who have never played the violin trying to teach each other how to do it, only a whole lot uglier.

Before we go any further, let's take a short test to see where you are now. This test will not be graded. It's more for us to know what you already know and what you need to know, so we can tell you, and then you'll know. Thinking like a terrorist, how would you answer these questions?

I _____ want to see anthrax spreading like a wildfire through the streets of America.
 A) Do not
 B) Greatly
 C) Kind of

I want to _____ my hands in the blood of infidels.
 A) Bathe
 B) Have no part in bathing
 C) Do lots of other things which are not bathing

Jihad is _____ under any ruler be he godly or wicked.
 A) Your duty
 B) An option to consider
 C) Never a good idea

واحتلت تشيلي المركز الثالث في البطولة التي اقيمت في كندب دعد فوزها علي النمسا بهدف مقابل ال شيء.
 A) الشباب ت
 B) استقت اهداف دعب
 C) لارجنتين

وبعد ديقيقتين تعادلت الارجنتين بهدف احرز هزرهم المهاجم as
 A) اجويرو هداف is to برصيد ديصرب is to استقت
 B) صانع العالب ال شيء. is to اللاع ب
 C) واحتلت تشيليي is to مقابل ال شيء

Hopefully, you did fairly well, but didn't answer all the questions correctly. If you scored well on the test, good for you—you're learning to think like a terrorist! If this test was too easy for you and you scored too well on it, you may be a terrorist. If you already are a terrorist, this chapter is probably not for you, since you already know how to think like a terrorist. Sorry we didn't put this note earlier, please feel free to skip to the next chapter.

OK, now we're sure that everybody reading this chapter, from here on anyway, is not a terrorist. So you're not a terrorist, and you're having trouble understanding the concept of a grudge held for 1,300 years. Imagine you're a Sunni. The ancestors of those Shiites in the next block did something bad to your ancestors 1,300 years ago. Of course you need to blow them up. It's a little like having five sons and pumping them all with growth hormones because you never made the NBA. Only in this case, the NBA is destruction of the state of Israel, and growth hormones are fundamentalist Islamic dogmatism. See? Don't forget to teach your children how to make free throws. Now, you're thinking like a terrorist.

But don't forget: you're not really a terrorist, you just think you are. Don't blow anything up.

Chapter 31A

Just for Terrorists—
If You're Not a
Terrorist, You Can
Skip This Chapter

You may have noticed that so far this book assumes that you, the terrorist, are a Muslim, probably from somewhere in the Middle East, though you might be from Pakistan, which isn't technically in the Middle East, but kind of nearby. But you may not be a Muslim, you might be a Basque terrorist, a narco-terrorist, a left-wing guerrilla, a member of a paramilitary death squad or an Irish terrorist. You may be in the ETA or the IRA or the PTA or the NHL, or you might even be an American Right Wing Christian Nut Case. But you're probably a Muslim, so for this chapter we're going to assume it. After all, the IRA is so 1980s.

The rest of this chapter will be written in your native tongue. It offers tips and techniques for making the transition from terrorist to non-terrorist. Also we address the issues that you care most about.

بعد شوط أول متواضع عرضى تقدم المنتخب التشيكي So
بهدف مرزه مارتن فنين من نينين تستديد رائعة في الدقيقة.
تبلق الجنتين تأخرها اماما تشيكيا روفزا، لتتمكن بذلك
من احراز بطولة كأس العالم لكرة القدم للشباب تحت عشرين عاما.

مجاهم الم هزرح ا ف دهب نين تنجنرالا ت الدا عت نين تقيقيدق ع بو
ق ريرمت د ع ب ف ادها ت ست ديصرب ةلوطبلا ف اده وريوجا وي جريس
ب يينيت من ص انع العا ب ا يفر ا ج يناج.

يف ت ميقا يت لا ةلوطبلا يف ث لاث لا زكرمل ا ليشت ت لتح او
ك ن دا ب ع د ف وزها على سم الم ن ف دهب ق اب ل ال ي ش ء.

ل غوت يت اراز ن كل يفاضا ت و قو ىل ت دمتست ةاراب مل ا نا ادب و
ن م ة يح يسلا ر اسر و خ عد و سرا حلا يك يش ت لا ك يدار ت يب رت
لل ار ج ن تي ن. ب ت ديدس ق قيوق ن م حافق ة قطنم ءا زجلا ارز ا ف دهل ا يناث

وج ءا رصن الا رجنت ن ين ع ن ق يرط لاع ب ها ر واروم ت اراز يذلا احرز
ف ده ف وزق لبق ع برا دق ا ئ اق ف قط ن م رف اص ةرف اتا نم تايكلت نوكتل
تجيتن ةارابم لا حالص ءانبا ا يريكلا يتاييت يي ن.

وب ذ لك ن وكت ن ين تنجنرالا دق ت زرزح تارم سمخ ب ق للا ت ارم يف
ن ن سخ سلا ع بس الا خ يرت ةلوطبلل.

ب ع د ش وط ل وا ى وتسم اضعم ىدقت ب خت ن م ل ا ت يش يك ي لا
ف دهب حزرم ن ت رام ن نيف ن من ديدس ت ة ع ئ ار يف الد ي قيقق.

ب ل ق ت ل ار ج نت ن ين ت أر خ ا ام ها ام ام ت ش ك ي ا ف وز ا، ت ل م ك ن ل ذ ل ك
ن م ا حارز ةلوطب ك س أ س ك ال ع الم ل ق رك ل د قم ل ا ب ش بل ا ت ح ع ر ش ن ي ن ا م ا.

مجاهم الم هزرح ا ف دهب نين تنجنرالا ت الدا عت نين تقيقيدق ع بو
ق ريرمت د ع ب ف ادها ت ست ديصرب ةلوطبلا ف اده وريوجا وي جريس
ب يينيت من ص انع العا ب ا يفر ا ج يناج.

و احلت ت ليشي ل ا زكرمل ا ث لاث ل ا
يف ةلوطب ل ا يت ا قيمت
يف ك ن دا ب ع د ف وزها على
ن م الم سم ف دهب ق اب ل ال ي ش ء.
و ةاراب مل ا ت ست مت د
ىل قو ت يفاضا نك ل يت اراز ل غوت
ن م يح يسلا ر اسر و خ عد و سرا حلا
ت لا ك يش يك يدار ت يب رت ب ت ديدس ق
ن م حافق ة قطنم ءا زجلا
ارز ا ف دهل ا يناث لل ار ج ن تي ن.
وج ءا رصن الا رجنت ن ين ع ن
ق يرط لاع ب ها ر واروم ت اراز يذلا
احرز ف ده ف وزق لبق ع برا دق ا ئ اق

ل كن ت اراز يت

فقط من صافرة الهنايةتي نتكلون نتيجة المبارارة لصالح ابناء
الكيرمي اللاتينيتة.

وبذلك نتكلون قد احرزت الارجنتينين قد احرزت اللقب خمس مرات في
النسخ السبع الخاخيرة للبطولة.

بعد شوط أول متوازي العضاء المستوى
تقدم المنتخب التشيكيي فدهـ
احرزه مارتن فينينن من تسديدة
رائعة في الدقيقة.

قلبت الارجنتينين أخرهها
تشيكيا فوزا، للتمكن
بذلك من احرزاز بطولة كأس
العالم لكرة القدم للشباب
تحت عشرين عاما. وبعد
دقيقتين تعادلت الارجنتينين.

التشيكيكي

بهدف مقابل الـ

■ الغسما ■ ربجق ■ بمجاربة
■ الجوديوخاني ■ فسي ■ انتطار

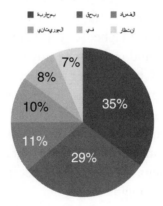

35%
29%
11%
10%
8%
7%

واحتلت تشيليي المركز الثالث في البطولة التي اقيمت في
كندا بعد فوزها على المنسا بهدف مقابل الـ شيء.

Q: وبدا ان المبارارة استمتدت الى قوى اضافيي لكن زارات توغل
من ناحية اليسار راس وخدع الحارس التشيكيي ديادري بيتر بتسديدة
قوية من على منطقة الجزاء محرز الهدف الثاني للارجنتين.

A: وجاء نصر الارجنتين عن طريق العبها رواور زارات الذي.

Chapter 32

Speaking to a Terrorist: How to Say "Naked Human Pyramid" in Arabic

Failures in communication are the leading causes of disagreement between the religions and races. If we could only learn to speak to one another, if there was a universal language, it's quite possible that there would be no religious wars, no ethnic hate, and maybe, just maybe, for once and for all, finally, the rest of the world would realize how silly their religions are and would accept Jesus Christ as their personal Lord and Savior. To help make this happen, we must learn to communicate with people we don't understand.

Sometimes you can use non-verbal communication with someone who doesn't speak your language. Various hand signals may be sufficient to express the most important ideas you want to convey to foreigners:

Yes

No

Stay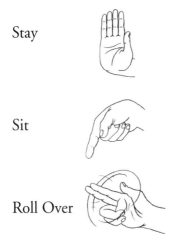

Sit

Roll Over

But some terrorists speak English. We invited aspiring terrorist Rashmir and white American dental assistant Jane to work on their communication skills under the guidance of a professional expert.

Jane: I'm feeling a little uncomfortable about the way Rashmir is looking at me, kind of like he wants to kill me—

Mediator: Rashmir, Jane is expressing a feeling of discomfort with the way you are looking at her. How do you react to that?

Rashmir: Americans are descendants of apes and pigs, who have been feeding from the dining tables of the Zionists.

Mediator: Rashmir, I'm wondering if you're recognizing Jane's uniqueness, or "lumping her together" with memories of past relationships. How do you feel right now towards Jane?

Rashmir: I am imagining cutting off her hands and slitting her throat so the blood runs down her belly, praise be Allah.

Jane: You see, that's exactly the kind of thing he would say, he's always threatening to cut off my hands and never thinking about how I feel, I just want him to *hear* me, not *fix* me.

Mediator: Rashmir, I don't really think you're hearing what Jane is trying to say to you. . . . You're invoking a defense mechanism, but not truly engaging her in open dialogue.

Rashmir: What man allows this woman to raise her eyes from the ground?

Mediator: Try not to put up a "defensive wall," but just listen to what Jane is communicating to you. Now Jane, is it possible that something you're doing could be contributing to the communication problems you're having with Rashmir?

Jane: I don't know, maybe. It just feels like when we have a problem to solve, it is like we are on opposite teams—like we're always just talking past each other.

Rashmir: You see? This is what happens when you let woman speak without ask permission. I should kill you both and make your youngest children a sacrifice gift for Allah.

Mediator: That's good Rashmir, I want you to give yourself permission to feel your negative emotions but without actually killing anyone, can we agree to that?

Rashmir: I guess.

Mediator: Jane, I want you to tell Rashmir how it makes you feel (without compartmentalizing your emotions!) when he threatens to kill you.

Jane: It makes me feel like he takes my presence for granted, like he doesn't value our relationship.

Mediator: Rashmir?

Rashmir: And they will know the true meaning when upon the earth a great fire consumes the nonbelievers and the boiling water will upon their—

Mediator: OK, I think we've made some real progress here today, and I look forward to our next session.

You're likely to find that even beyond the language barrier, there are other barriers. Here's the situation: you're at a gathering of the local PTA, the Ku Klux Klan, or some other pleasant social event, and you find yourself making small talk with someone your gut tells you is a terrorist. What to do?

Most of us find it hard enough to make small talk with someone we don't know well, to say nothing of a religious fanatic dedicated to the murder of all freedom-loving white people.

A couple of Don'ts: Don't try to ingratiate yourself with him by talking about the return of the caliphate and how nice that would be. Don't just blurt out, "God is great!" "There is no god but God," or "Death to the Great Satan!" It's not going to sound "right" coming from you.

A couple of Do's: Do try to be casual, ask which team he likes in the next World Cup, how much you admire the modesty of Arab women, and how we could benefit from a religious police right here in America. With this kind of light chatter you're less likely to tip him off to your suspicions, while gaining his trust.

Q: Does any of this relate to the next chapter?

A: Probably not, but let's take a look!

Chapter 33

Ethics in the Post-Geneva Convention Era

Ethics, morals, scruples, ubiquitous, libertarian: what do these words really mean? Nobody actually knows, we just say them a lot when we're trying to make an argument against something we don't like, because people then think we know what we're talking about when we really don't. So instead of running around using words that we don't know what they mean, why don't we take the time to create definitions that we can all agree on and live with?

For example, let's define ethics as the delicate balance between what we want to do and what we will get yelled at for doing by the ACLU; Libertarian as kind of like a new college student struggling with his/her sexuality, while failing out of freshman year; and morals as large, slippery, saltwater-dwelling, eel-like creatures that feed on small fish and algae and sometimes glow. With these concrete definitions in mind, we can begin to look at specific issues that people complain about, using words like ethics, morals, and ubiquitous and see if their arguments make any sense.

For example, some people say that it should be against our morals to imprison people indefinitely without a trial, a lawyer, or any sort of charges being brought against them. But knowing now what we know about morals being an ocean-based eel-type thing, we realize that whoever was making that argument is not only wrong, but possibly a little bit insane.

In this chapter we will look at places like Guantanamo, Abu Ghraib, and your own personal detention facilities and analyze whether or not they are moral, ethical, and ubiquitous.

Q: That sounds really boring. Can we do something else?

A: What would you like to do?

Q: How about a game? We haven't played any games in a while.

A: You mean like a kid's game?

Q: No. An adult game.

A: OK. Let's play, *The Ultimate Counterterrorist Home Companion* Drinking Game. First, turn on Fox News. Now: every time you hear any of the following words or phrases everybody has to take a drink.

"War on Terror"

"Cut and run."

"Shut up, shut up."

"And now with more insightful commentary: Ann Coulter."

(Note: the home version of this game has more quotes, but during the test run, there were several cases of alcohol poisoning in the focus groups for people who played this game for more than 30 minutes. Lawyers have advised us to reduce the game to just these four quotes.)

Q: Are you going to get around to talking about the Geneva Convention?

A: You didn't like the drinking game?

Q: Not really. But the Geneva Convention sounds cool. Is that like a bunch of sales reps getting together for a few days out of town, hiring prostitutes, and drinking?

A: No. The Geneva Convention is a serious agreement amongst the nations of the world regarding the rules of war and the treatment of prisoners, which was written by terrorists.

Here are some of the provisions of the treaty, originally written in French but translated below:

Section IV, Subsection 2, Paragraph 3: Terrorist prisoners must not be tortured.

Section IX, Subsection 5, Paragraph 2: Each terrorist prisoner will be offered a wide variety of dinner options. If none of the options are pleasing, he shall have the right to be served whatever food he wants. All meals shall come with a vanilla, chocolate, or strawberry shake.

Section XXV, Subsection 8, Paragraph 14: Each terrorist is entitled to one back rub or foot message each day at sundown.

In summary, the Geneva Convention is no longer useful, and French people are a bunch of assholes. In the post-Geneva Convention era, we need to make our own rules for morals and ethics. But since you haven't been patient with this topic, we're going to move on to religion, without which morals and ethics could not exist. But first,

Kidz Korner

Help GI Joe Get Out of This Hole!
Choose the best option for GI Joe:

Jibby   Koko

a) dig deeper
b) dig faster
d) surge
e) dig another hole
    someplace else
f) stay the dig
g) dig the course

Chapter 34

Religious Chapter

You know how in the ancient times, kings, dukes, and royal folk of all sorts would have religious awakenings on their deathbed, and suddenly become totally pious for like three days and give all their riches to the church in a desperate attempt to have the higher powers forgive their lifetime worth of sins, while conveniently screwing their ungrateful offspring all at the same time?

Well, we here are on the deathbed of this book and are also suddenly realizing we may have overlooked the importance of religion in our lives, and will now generously donate everything we have left in sheep, slaves, and chapters to the subject of religion in a desperate attempt to be forgiven for all of the chapters leading up to this one. And to all higher powers reading this, don't be offended that it came so late in the book. The end of the book is actually just as important as the beginning of the book, especially if you flip it over and read it backwards.

More to the point, religion is a major driving force behind the worldwide spread of terrorism. And not just the obvious one. There are actually many different religions in the world (more than four less than eight) and it is important that we familiarize ourselves briefly with them all if we are to ever truly understand whatever it is we were talking about at the beginning of this paragraph.

All the major world's religions are related, not in the way brothers and sisters are related, but in the way you and some distant cousin who have been sworn enemies involved in a multigenerational family feud then one day realize you have a

154 The Ultimate Counterterrorist Home Companion

common great aunt are related. Therefore, even though the terrorists themselves are not Judeo-Christians, it's important to discuss the Judeo-Christian religions.

The Judeo-Christian Religions

What a shame it is that the world's best religions, those which have just one God (more or less) have been used by terrorists to justify their acts of violence. Doesn't it make you want to kill somebody?

The oldest (not necessarily the best!) of the Judeo-Christian religions is Judaism, the religion of the Jews. The Jewish people do not accept Our Savior, and unfortunately for them, will be going straight to Hell. This isn't our fault, since they've had ample opportunity to accept Christ. Anyway, their Bible is the Old Testament, which is a very peaceful holy book. For example, the Ten Commandments, which believe it or not, was a Jew idea!

The Fifth Commandment, which is very highly ranked,[2] says: Thou Shalt Not Kill. Now that is pretty peaceful. You'd never know that Jews (at one time) planned to eat Christian children.

After that, of course, comes the actual Bible. This is sometimes called "The New Testament" as a kind of "stop" sign for Jews, in case they accidentally keep reading past their own "old" book and end up being saved!

The other cool thing about the emergence of the Judeo-Christian religions is that we moved past the pagan religions, which had many gods whose names were hard to remember, and who were also drunken sexual predators. While this may be a fun quality to have in a college roommate, it's not a good quality in a god. The only time the real God had sex with a woman was

---

[2] Right after the ones about how there will be no "seeing other Gods" whether or not you "need more space," how you shouldn't swear, you should do what your parents tell you to do, you shouldn't have any graven images or worship them if you happen to find one, you shouldn't work on Saturday (which is Jewish for Sunday) or even let your slave work on Saturday (Sunday).

specifically for the purpose of giving to us His Only Begotten Son, to save us from Hell. And there was no partying involved.

But let's get some information from a primary source. We talked to a surprise guest to get an inside look at the War on Terror from a religious point of view.

Interview with Jesus

The Ultimate Counterterrorist Home Companion sat down with Jesus last Thursday afternoon.

*Jesus Christ, 33, is Our Lord and Savior, and coauthor of **The New Testament**, a bestseller. He lives with his parents in the sky.*

TUCHC: Do you think going into Iraq was a good idea?

JC: I do support the action, but I would have done it differently. I would have gone in with sufficient troops to secure the peace.

TUCHC: Yes or no: Do you love the terrorists?

JC: It's kind of a love-hate relationship.

TUCHC: What do you think about pre-emptive war?

JC: I think a responsible savior would never take any options off the table.

TUCHC: Would you condone torture if you believed a detainee had knowledge of an imminent attack that could kill hundreds of American citizens?

JC: Let me say that I know a little about torture, and it's just not an effective means of getting accurate information. On the other hand, what the heck, it's worth a try, right?

TUCHC: Is the War on Terrorism a religious war in your opinion?

JC: On the record—I would say it's a war of ideas, a struggle to spread good information and increase communication.

TUCHC: Off the record?

JC: Off the record? Screw those camel-blowing, Godless pricks. You're damn right it's a religious war, and I ain't gonna lose.

TUCHC: What's with that "discovering Jesus' tomb" show? Was that legit? 'Cause it was pretty convincing.

JC: Sorry, didn't see it, haven't got TiVo yet and Tuesday is always *24* night in my house. Hey, can I use the bathroom?

TUCHC: Just a couple more questions.

JC: But I really gotta go.

TUCHC: We're almost done here. Has the War on Terror made us more or less safe?

JC: Who's "us," white boy? I'm already dead, I ain't worried.

TUCHC: Do you think we will be hit again?

JC: You all have to be right 100% of the time, they only have to be right once. Being right 100% of the time is easy for me, I'm God. But for you people . . . I'd give you maybe a few more years.

TUCHC: About that, forgive me, but I just don't understand. Are you God, or are you His Son, or are you both God, or what, 'cause I thought there was really only supposed to be one?

JC: He's God, I'm God, we're both God, just deal with it, OK? Are you going to give me a hard time here?

TUCHC: What's up with that Mary Magdalene chick? Did you ever . . . you know . . .

JC: That's a little personal, don't you think?

TUCHC: Well you are a personal lord and savior.

JC: Not that personal.

TUCHC: Is the War on Terror really just a big distraction from the real crucial issues of our time, like global warming, nuclear proliferation, starvation, AIDS, etc.?

JC: Whatever keeps you people busy.

TUCHC: All right Jesus, keep it real baby, much love.

JC: Peace out.

Divine Literary Intervention

It's a good idea if you're fighting them here or over there, to carry a Holy Bible with you at all times, because it's well known that Bibles have stopped bullets, and it's cheaper than body armor. Also recommended, *Slander* by Ann Coulter.

And speaking of going to Hell, there's the most misunderstood of all the Big Three Religions. It's so misunderstood that it deserves its very own chapter in some other book. It also deserves its own chapter so that nobody confuses it with the Judeo-Christian religions, which it is definitely not one of. But here it won't get its own chapter, just its own section.

The Islamo-Fascist Religions

The truth about the Islamo-Fascist religions is that they're not as bad as their name would suggest. These religions, unfortunately, have been hijacked by extremists. The actual document from which these religions are formed, the Koran, is at its core a peaceful and loving text. Anyway, at least they believe in something. It's the Atheists we should really be afraid of. If the Islamic peoples can find a way to bring out the true meaning of the Koran, the world will be a much more harmonious place, and the eventual global takeover by Christianity will be a lot more pleasant for everyone.

So let's take a look at the Koran to discover its core values. Here are some important quotes reminding us of its loving nature:

When the forbidden months are past, then fight and slay the pagans wherever ye find them, and seize them, beleaguer them, and lie in wait for them in every stratagem (of war) for the Prophet said:

Seek the paths of peace and do not wage war against God and His Apostle.

The punishment of those who wage war against God and His Apostle, and strive with might and main for mischief through the land is execution, or crucifixion, or the cutting off of hands and feet from opposite sides, or exile from the land.

In order that Allah may separate the impure from the pure, Put All the impure ones (Non-Muslim), one on top of another in a Heap and cast them into Hell.

But when you have a moment, remember that God is a loving God, and thou shall love thy friends and also thine enemies.

Speaking of thine enemies: Smite ye above their necks and smite all their fingertips off them. Like the boiling of scalding water Seize Ye Him and drag him into the midst of the blazing Fire. Then pour over his head the penalty of Boiling Water.

Righteous women are devoutly obedient, and guard in (the husband's) absence what God would have them guard. As to those women on whose part ye fear disloyalty and ill conduct, admonish them (first), (Next), refuse to share their beds, (And last) beat them (lightly).

Remember that women should be respected and treated well at all times.

Unless they doeth unto their husband/masters a thing which he deemeth to be unpleasing, at which point she should be admonished, beaten or subject to whatever punishment he, the master, should see fit.

Q: How come you had a nice illustration of Jesus, but no illustration of Mohammed?

A: We were going to have one of Mohammed, but it was supposed to be a surprise. Now we can't put one in. You've ruined it for everyone.

Thank you for reading this book. You are now ready for the final exam.

SPECIAL ALERT!

Final Exam

---

1) True or False: I skipped right to the end of the book without reading it first to take this exam.

2) I did this because:
    A) I'm an intellectually curious person.
    B) It's the closest thing to cheating available in the book.
    C) Hey! It's not cheating! It's in all the how-to study guides.

3) When did you stop plotting terrorist attacks against the U.S.?
    A) Oh, a long time ago.
    B) Never! I mean always!
    C) Is this a trick question?

4) We're asking the questions.

6) Why didn't you answer question number 5?

7) Well, you're not being very cooperative. But we'll move ahead, while making a note of your behavior. Terrorism is to jihad *as:*
    A) Attitude :: Conundrum
    B) Milk shake :: The Green Bay Packers
    C) Salamander :: The Cosmological Constant

Hmmm. You didn't do very well on the test. Remember, if you're not sure of the answer to question number five, it's still better to take an educated guess. But it would help if you read the book first.

Q: Well, that was a very educational and informative book. I enjoyed it a lot.

A: Thank you. You, too, have helped with your provocative questions.

Appendix

All the Boring Stuff You Don't Have to Read

Further Reading Suggestions

In deciding what books you will read, it can be helpful to know the general level of ultimateness that the book contains. For example, if you were considering reading another book on this subject, or another book on any subject, you would probably want to know if it was more or less ultimate than this book that you have already read. If you know that the other books are less ultimate, you can save yourself the trouble of reading them and just re-read this one. For this purpose, we have analyzed the contents of this book and various others that you might be interested in reading and have assessed, fairly and scientifically, their respective ultimatenesses.

Measurable Ultimateness Comparison Chart

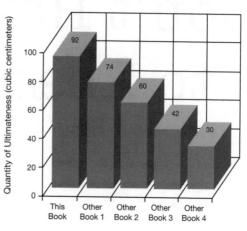

About the Authors

Larry Arnstein worked at the CIA as an undercover agent for many years until his cover was blown by Dick Cheney after a shouting match at a pickup basketball game. Currently, he holds the Dennis Rodman Chair of National Securities Studies at Borden State University, where he is a Visiting Professor of Panic.

Zack Arnstein has personally killed over eight terrorists that he found in his own neighborhood. Or at least he thinks they were terrorists. . . . He's pretty damn sure, actually. Yeah, they definitely had to be terrorists. Probably. He is currently completing his doctorate, also at Borden State, in epiosteemiology.

This is their third book. While they have a common last name, they are not related, nor do they interact socially. Their previous books are:

The Dog Ate My Resumé:
Survival Tips for Life After College

The Bad Driver's Handbook:
Hundreds of Simple Maneuvers to Frustrate, Annoy, and Endanger Those Around You

About Borden State University (Authors' Place of Work and Study)

Founded in 1898 as an agricultural college by Elsie Borden and conveniently located on the border between Missouri and Virginia, BSU has become a respected center of higher learning in engineering, science, and the humanities, attracting students and graduate students from around the globe.

Still respecting tradition, BSU welcomes cows to its campus, where they can be seen wandering the fields, lawns, halls, and classrooms, mingling freely with students and faculty.

It is from this tradition that BSU sports teams derive their name, The Cow Pies. Indeed, last year The Cow Pies won the coveted Salt Lick Trophy at the Cud Bowl, and with it another banner to fly atop Elsie Borden Stadium. Alumni are still buzzing about the game, where, spurred on by the excited "Moo-o-o-o, moo-o-o-o, moo, moo, moo!" cheers of a frenzied crowd, The Cow Pies won the game on a quarterback sneak, scoring as time ran out on the last play. The picture on sports pages the following day of the field mobbed with joyous players, fans, and cows speaks for itself.